Sunbonnet
FAMILY REUNION
126 WINNING DESIGNS WITH COMPLETE INSTRUCTIONS

Album IV

Copyright © 1991 House of White Birches, 306 East Parr Road, Berne, Indiana 46711.

ALL RIGHTS RESERVED. No part of this book may be reproduced in any form or by any means without the prior written permission of the publisher, excepting brief quotes in connection with reviews written specifically for inclusion in a magazine or newspaper.

Library of Congress Catalog Number: 89-81185
ISBN: 1-882138-02-3

Sunbonnet Family Reunion, Album IV

Editor: Sandra Hatch
Art Director/Writer: Ken Tate
Artist: Janice Tate
Design Coordinator: Jeanie Czarnecki
Production Assistants: Carol Dailey, Cathy Reef
Photography: Rhonda Davis, Nancy Sharp, Mary Joynt, Kay Weller

House of White Birches

Publishers: Carl H. Muselman
Arthur K. Muselman

Chief Executive Officer: John Robinson
Marketing Director: Scott Moss
Editorial Coordinator: Vivian Potratz Rothe
Products Manager: Beth Schwartz
Circulation Manager: Carole Butler
Production Coordinator: Sandra Ridgway
Newsstand Consultant: Angelo Gandino

Every effort has been made to have patterns and instructions in *Sunbonnet Family Reunion, Album IV* as accurate as possible. However, we cannot be responsible for human errors, typographical mistakes or problems you might encounter in constructing these pieces. Most of these patterns are original designs. We have attempted to accurately credit those few that are adaptations of previously published patterns.

Welcome to *Sunbonnet Family Reunion Album IV*, the final book in our series. If you missed our first three reunions, you might want to complete your collection by referring to the ordering information given on the last pages of this book.

My favorite patterns in this book are those showing Sue quilting. And the cover, which is a quilter's rendition of an original Bertha Corbett design, makes a beautiful block. Its maker, Norma N. Locke, won the Bertha Corbett Award in the Sunbonnet Family Reunion contest.

The Sunbonnet contest block exhibit is still traveling the country. Thousands of people have viewed it and have come away with such a good feeling. Much like a family reunion, this old and popular pattern theme stirs up good feelings in all of us.

Read about the sponsors of the contest that prompted the development of the reunions, as well as about Bertha Corbett, the acknowledged creator of the original Sunbonnet children back in the early 1900s. Turn the pages to get a feeling of what the patterns are and then really look at each one to find one you'd like to try. I imagine you won't be able to choose just one but will want to make a sampler with all of your favorites. It's more fun that way anyway. As you begin to copy the pattern, choose your fabrics and begin to sew, you will be beginning your own family reunion for future generations to attend. Each person who looks at your quilt will ask questions about your creation and the lucky owners will have small reunions of their own held around these stories. It's important to write up a legend to attach to your quilt so 100 years from now it will be known who made it and when. More information can be written down as well, such as who it was made for and for what occasion—the more information, the better.

Reunions are happy times—times to recollect, reacquaint yourselves and see how far you've come. Our *Sunbonnet Family Reunions* have been fun and have taken us back to simpler times, but have also shown us our present and a little of our future. We know that Sunbonnet Sue patterns are part of that quilting future no matter what the date. She's a timeless tradition that quilters will want to hold onto forever.

Sandra L. Hatch

Sunbonnet

	PAGE		PAGE
Introduction	2	Family 11 Patterns	124
Bertha L. Corbett	4	Family 12 Patterns	133
Dorothymae and Harold Groves	5	Family 13 Patterns	143
Family 1	7	Family 14 Patterns	152
Family 2	8	Cover Design	162
Family 3	9	Index	164
Family 4	10		
Family 5	11		
Family 6	12		
Family 7	13		
Family 8	14		
Family 9	15		
Family 10	16		
Family 11	17		
Family 12	18		
Family 13	19		
Family 14	20		
General Instructions	21		
Family 1 Patterns	25		
Family 2 Patterns	35		
Family 3 Patterns	44		
Family 4 Patterns	53		
Family 5 Patterns	64		
Family 6 Patterns	73		
Family 7 Patterns	82		
Family 8 Patterns	91		
Family 9 Patterns	102		
Family 10 Patterns	113		

About Our Cover...

Our cover quilt piece, *Painting*, was designed and appliquéd by Norma N. Locke of Gaston, Ore. Norma's block earned her the Bertha Corbett Award and a prize in the first Sunbonnet Family Reunion, sponsored by Groves Publishing Company of Kansas City. She was one of over 40 prizewinners in the contest. Norma's prizewinning pattern may be found on page 162 of this edition.

FAMILY REUNION
126 WINNING DESIGNS WITH COMPLETE INSTRUCTIONS

Bertha L. Corbett
Mother of the Sunbonnet Babies

Quilters have long known that quilting is a form of art.

What quilter hasn't felt the onrush of creative spirit as she sat down to her work? It then seems only natural that an artist would contribute much to the art of quiltmaking.

Such is the story of Bertha L. Corbett Melcher, the "Mother of the Sunbonnet Babies."

Bertha Corbett began her career in Minneapolis, Minn., and later spent a year of training with illustrator Howard Pyle. It was during her time in Minneapolis, around the turn of the century, that Bertha conceived the idea of her Babies and proved they were not just another pretty face.

In fact, they had no faces at all.

During a social gathering of several artist friends, one observed that a faceless figure displays little emotional expression. Bertha remembered seeing a small girl, her face hidden by a large sunbonnet. The child's faceless beauty caused her to remark, "I don't think a face is necessary in order to make a figure expressive." Challenged to prove her point by the other artists, Bertha picked up her pen and drew her first Sunbonnet Baby.

Bertha's work so captivated the artists and, later, a growing group of admirers, that she began to devote more and more of her time to her nursery of characters. First a book and then a children's primer were produced to satisfy people's hunger for more and more of the Babies.

Later, Bertha — who also wrote much of the verse accompanying the illustrations — turned the concept into a popular comic strip.

She also became a popular guest on the lecture and vaudeville circuit.

On one visit to Los Angeles, Bertha spoke at social and professional functions and delivered several lectures on her creation. At all these functions she sported what one newspaper called her "quaint conceit... a stick pin mounted with a tiny medallion showing her trademark — a bewitching little sunbonnet baby a quarter of an inch long."

Bertha was described as "a slender, brown-haired girl with a face filled with animation, expressive eyes and a smile at once frank and winning. She loves children or she could never draw them so sympathetically and charmingly as she does, so that every woman who looks at one wants to take it up in her arms and cuddle it."

The Babies seemed to take on a life of their own. They became the subject of holiday greeting cards. They adorned advertising and promotional material, including the popular — and still marketed — Dutch Cleanser®. Bertha often joked that she expected a visit from the Labor Commission because, "the babies are so very young to be made to earn a living for me."

Bertha made two moral stipulations for the use of her Babies in the earning of her living: "One was that my sunbonnet babies shall never be guilty of being saucy to their elders, and the other was that they should never under any circumstances be spanked!"

Soon "Overall Boys" began to accompany the Sunbonnet Girls to all important functions. Together, the pair, in all their various sizes and shapes, were shown in almost every conceivable childhood activity and chore.

The revival of interest in Bertha Corbett's work came about through the labors of some of the country's best quilt designers. The faceless children have a timeless quality about them, the perfect qualification for quilting. So, in addition to all of the Sunbonnet memorabilia being collected and printed, there is also a continual interest in the Babies as quilting models.

It is fitting that the work of Bertha Corbett be recognized in the quilting world. Through her art at the turn of the last century, the art of quilting has been elevated to new heights as we near the turn of this century.

By Ken Tate

Dorothymae and Harold Groves
Sunbonnet Entrepreneurs

Sunbonnet Girls and Overall Boys are a way of life for Dorothymae and Harold Groves of Kansas City.

The Groves, who conceived, compiled and now are touring the Sunbonnet Family Reunion contest, have become sunbonnet entrepreneurs in their own right. In addition to the contest, Harold and Dorothymae operate Groves Publishing Company, specializing in Sunbonnet memorabilia.

Their wares include 11 reprinted books of Bertha L. Corbett Melcher, Sunbonnet greeting cards, plus dozens of pieces of Sunbonnet gift items. Additionally, Harold compiled the *Kansas City Star's* classic quilt patterns in ten volumes.

Dorothymae's love of Sunbonnet Babies began with sunbonnet tole paintings in 1968, painted for the couple's

Continued on next page

three daughters. In 1982, she quilted her first Sunbonnet Baby quilt from a top pieced by her late mother-in-law.

In 1988, the couple began collecting postcards, ink blotters, calendars, books and dishes of sunbonnets. They now have over 330 postcards dated from 1903 to the 1920s, with many in complete series.

The high point of Dorothymae's involvement with sunbonnets came in July 1989, when she spent three days with Ruth Melcher Thom, the second daughter of Bertha Corbett Melcher.

The Groves compiled 504 Sunbonnet quilt designs for the *Sunbonnet Family Reunion*. The blocks came from entrants from 6 to 83 years of age. In addition to entries from the United States and Canada, the Groves received blocks from the Netherlands and Australia.

Dorothymae says her love of Sunbonnets stems from the fact that, because the Babies' faces never show, there is no connection of racial, ethnic or national characteristics to them, making them "international quilt figures."

She also says the quilts and their models "make you smile without seeing a smile."

Dorothymae is a recognized quilter in her own right. In addition to many "best of show" ribbons at state fairs, she has also seen one of her quilts displayed at Disneyland.

Dorothymae says she could never have completed the work on the Sunbonnet Family Reunion contest without the help of Harold, who not only built the display panels, but also ironed each of the blocks for mounting for the tour and exhibit.

Harold travels with Dorothymae to virtually all the shows she attends. The Groves have taken the Reunion exhibit to over a dozen sites, with several more planned.

They are also planning the next Reunion contest, scheduled for the summer and fall of 1990.

Sunbonnet FAMILY REUNION — FAMILY 1

"I don't think a face is necessary in order to make a figure expressive."
—Bertha L. Corbett

Poetry excerpts from *The Sunbonnet Babies* by Bertha Corbett, reprinted by Groves Publishing Company, Kansas City, Mo.

See Page 25	See Page 26	See Page 27
See Page 28	See Page 29	See Page 31
See Page 32	See Page 33	See Page 34

Sunbonnet Family Reunion IV 7

See Page 35	See Page 36	See Page 37
See Page 38	See Page 39	See Page 40
See Page 41	See Page 42	See Page 43

FAMILY 2

Sunbonnet FAMILY REUNION

Of course we've many calls to pay
So we go out each pleasant day.

8 Sunbonnet Family Reunion IV

Sunbonnet FAMILY 3
FAMILY REUNION

Bright has dawned the picnic day,
And we sally forth quite gay.

See Page 44	See Page 45	See Page 46
See Page 47	See Page 48	See Page 49
See Page 50	See Page 51	See Page 52

Sunbonnet Family Reunion IV

See Page 53	See Page 55	See Page 56
See Page 57	See Page 58	See Page 59
See Page 60	See Page 61	See Page 63

FAMILY 4

Sunbonnet FAMILY REUNION

When the washing all is done
Hang the clothes up in the sun.

Sunbonnet Family Reunion IV

Sunbonnet FAMILY REUNION — FAMILY 5

With bent pins we wait for fish
But no bites answer our wish.

See Page 64	See Page 65	See Page 66
See Page 67	See Page 68	See Page 69
See Page 70	See Page 71	See Page 72

Sunbonnet Family Reunion IV

See Page 73	See Page 74	See Page 75
See Page 76	See Page 77	See Page 78
See Page 79	See Page 80	See Page 81

FAMILY 6 — Sunbonnet FAMILY REUNION

Now when the morning comes they wake and start at once to mend,

12 Sunbonnet Family Reunion IV

Sunbonnet FAMILY 7
FAMILY REUNION

For on their needle handiwork their dollies must depend.

See Page 82	See Page 83	See Page 84
See Page 85	See Page 86	See Page 87
See Page 88	See Page 89	See Page 90

Sunbonnet Family Reunion IV 13

See Page 91	See Page 93	See Page 94
See Page 95	See Page 96	See Page 97
See Page 98	See Page 99	See Page 100

FAMILY 8 Sunbonnet FAMILY REUNION

The Sunbonnet Babies lived, you know,
In this little ink-bottle round and low,
And I helped them out, with the aid of a pen—

14 Sunbonnet Family Reunion IV

Sunbonnet FAMILY REUNION **FAMILY 9**

See Page 102	See Page 103	See Page 104
See Page 105	See Page 106	See Page 108
See Page 109	See Page 110	See Page 112

So you might see, all through the book
The things they did, and the way they look.

Sunbonnet Family Reunion IV 15

See Page 113	See Page 115	See Page 116
See Page 117	See Page 118	See Page 119
See Page 120	See Page 121	See Page 123

FAMILY 10 — Sunbonnet FAMILY REUNION

Gardens in the Spring we make,
Clear the ground with hoe and rake.

16 Sunbonnet Family Reunion IV

Sunbonnet FAMILY 11
FAMILY REUNION

Plant them nicely in a row
So that they will quickly grow.

See Page 124	See Page 125	See Page 126
See Page 127	See Page 128	See Page 129
See Page 130	See Page 131	See Page 132

Sunbonnet Family Reunion IV 17

See Page 133	See Page 134	See Page 136
See Page 137	See Page 138	See Page 139
See Page 140	See Page 141	See Page 142

Family 12 Sunbonnet FAMILY REUNION

See the little chicks we feed;
Such a lot of care they need.

18 Sunbonnet Family Reunion IV

Sunbonnet FAMILY REUNION · FAMILY 13

Sometimes we dress up in the style
And play at "Lady" for awhile.

See Page 143	See Page 144	See Page 145
See Page 146	See Page 147	See Page 148
See Page 149	See Page 150	See Page 151

Sunbonnet Family Reunion IV

See Page 152	See Page 153	See Page 154
See Page 155	See Page 156	See Page 158
See Page 159	See Page 160	See Page 161

FAMILY 14 Sunbonnet FAMILY REUNION

"Sunbonnet Babies shall never be guilty of being saucy to their elders, and they shall never, under any circumstances, be spanked."

—Bertha L. Corbett

20 Sunbonnet Family Reunion IV

Sunbonnet
FAMILY REUNION
General Instructions

All but one of the blocks shown in this book are appliqued designs. Each block was designed to fit a 12" background square. If you want a larger block, you may enlarge the pattern as desired.

Applique is the process of applying one piece of fabric on top of another for decorative or functional purposes. The functional purpose is generally in the form of a patch to cover a damaged portion of a garment or other fabric covering. Decorative applique can be part of clothing, quilts, pillows, furniture and most any other fabric item that might need a bit of design or color to brighten it.

Applique is popular because one can almost paint pictures with the fabric pieces. Flowers, animals, architecture and even human faces can be portrayed in fabric through the process of applique. Piecing can result in some of the same designs, but the look is not the same. Applique is rich and flowing.

Before the actual applique begins, the background block needs to be cut (at least 1/2" larger all around than desired finished size) and prepared for stitching. Most applique designs are centered on the block in some manner. To find the center of your background square, fold in half, and in half again, and crease with your fingers. Now unfold and fold diagonally and crease again. Repeat for other corners.

You now have a block with center-line creases to help you position your design. Some people just like to place their pieces as they wish, but others like to be very precise. If you have a full-size drawing of your design, as is given with the Sunbonnets in this book, you might like to draw the design on your background block to help with placement. This is most easily accomplished by first transferring the design to a large piece of paper. Tracing paper would be the easiest kind to use. Place paper on top of the design and, using masking tape, tape to hold in place. Trace design onto paper.

If you have a light box, the next step would be easy. Many people do not have one of these helpful devices. Inventive quilters have found that a large window works almost as well. Stand up close and tape your pattern on the window while you trace your design onto your background block with a water-erasable marker or chalk pencil. This drawing will show you exactly where your fabric pieces should be placed on your background block.

Once your design has been transferred to your background, you must prepare templates for each shape that requires applique. Templates are made for each piece by tracing off shapes one at a time. You should use something stiff for this step — cardboard or plastic template material made especially for this purpose may be used. Draw the shape of your design onto your template material. If you are accustomed to using templates with seam allowance added, at this time, draw another line around your shape 1/4" away from the first line. For machine applique, a seam allowance is not necessary. Most hand appliquers prefer to leave the seam allowance off the template and add it to the shape during the cutting process. Cut out the template on your drawn line.

There are many techniques one can use to applique. The most traditional is hand applique. The preferred method is to use a template made from the desired finished shape without seam allowance added. Fabrics are chosen (100 percent cotton is recommended) and prewashed to prevent the bleeding of color to the background block once the block is finished. When prewashing is done and the fabric has been ironed, trace the desired shape onto the right side of the fabric with a water-erasable marker, light lead or white chalk pencil. Leave at least 1/2" between design motifs when tracing to allow for the seam allowance when cutting out your shapes. When the desired number of shapes needed have been drawn on your fabric pieces, cut out shapes leaving 1/8" - 1/4" all around drawn line for turning under. Some applique experts advise you to stitch around the shape just outside the turning line to give you a guide for the turning line. This keeps the piece from stretching out of shape as you work with it. This is an optional step.

Freezer paper applique has been popular in recent years. The purpose of using freezer paper is to help you make your shape conform exactly to the shape of the template used for your design. Cut the finished shape out of freezer paper and iron the shiny side onto the wrong side of fabric. Cut out shape 1/4" larger around paper pattern, clip curves and iron seam allowances under. Remove paper before applique if desired, or leave inside during applique process and remove by pulling through a small opening left at the end before final stitches are taken, or by cutting away background from back and pulling the paper from underneath when block is finished. The English paper-piecing method is done in a similar fashion, except, in many of the older quilts, the paper was never removed when the quilt was completed.

If you do not use paper as a guide for turning your edges under and making smooth shapes, you might want to turn your shape's edges over on the drawn or stitched line (if you machine stitched around your design). When turning the edges under, remember to make sharp corners sharp and smooth edges smooth. Your fabric patch should retain the shape of the template used to cut it.

Basting the edges over may be helpful to some stitchers. When the edges are basted over before the actual applique process, the shape is already formed and it does help to make the process easier. Some stitchers prefer to turn the edge under with their needle as they work rather than take the time necessary for hand basting. Experiment with several methods and choose the one that works best for you or invent one of your own!

Machine applique can be as beautiful as hand applique but in some circumstances this is not easy to accomplish. There are several new products available to help make the process easier and faster.

Some stitchers advocate the use of a product called Wonder Under® by Pellon. This product has paper on one side. To use, dry-iron it onto the wrong side of your fabric. Draw desired shapes onto the paper and cut them out. Peel off paper, position on the right side of your background block and dry-iron in place. Your shape will stay in place until you have machine stitched all around it. This process does add a little bulk or stiffness to the appliqued shape and may make quilting through the layers by hand more difficult.

Another product that helps make applique easier and stabilizes your background fabric is called Stitch-N-Tear®. This is placed under the background fabric while machine applique is being done, and then torn away when work is finished. This kind of stabilizer helps to keep the background fabric from pulling during the machine applique process.

During the actual applique process, you will be layering one shape on top of another. Where two fabrics overlap, the underneath piece does not have to be turned under or stitched down. If possible, the underneath fabric should be trimmed away when block is finished. This is done by carefully cutting away the background from underneath and then cutting away unnecessary layers. Quilting through several layers by hand is not an easy process.

After positioning fabric shapes on your background block, pin or baste them in place. Using a blind or applique stitch, sew pieces in place with matching thread and small stitches. Start with background pieces first and work up to foreground pieces. If you would like to add dimension to your pieces, a bit of stuffing may be inserted in a piece before the final stitches are made. Be sure that the stuffing is distributed evenly before final stitches are made. Do not cut away background fabric from beneath stuffed areas.

The patterns given in this book require some added detail work with embroidery stitches. Many shapes are too small to be appliqued but are integral parts of the design. These shapes are added with embroidery floss. If you refer to the colored photograph of each block, you will be able to see the details. In some cases, they could be eliminated, if you prefer not to add them. However, these little details do add a great deal to the finished looks of the blocks. Diagrams of the most common stitches are given here. Color and stitch recommendations may be changed to suit your own stitching tastes.

Special shapes require special skills. The diagrams shown provide some extra help in successful completion of applique of these shapes. Be sure to refer to this guide, as well as the color photographs at the beginning of this book when working on your blocks.

Applique Stitch Guide

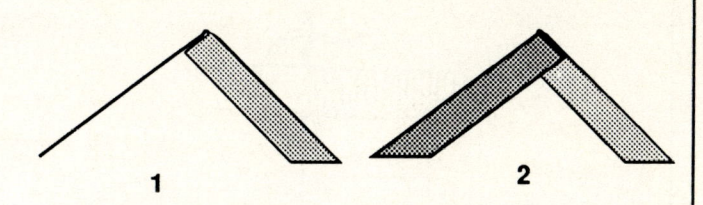

Corners: To make a neat square corner, fold in one edge of your piece 1/4" or on seam line to the wrong side, then fold over second edge. For corners that have very pointed edges, such as a leaf, fold down tip first, then fold in sides; excess fabric might need to be trimmed.

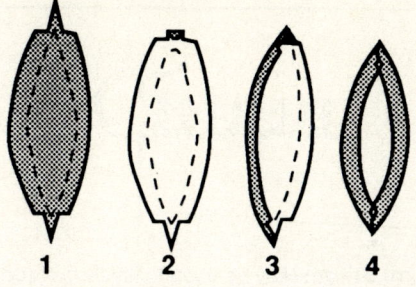

Pointed Corners: Clip off seam allowance to 1/8" below point. Fold point over at tip to seam allowance. Fold in trimmed sides at seam line. This method is most commonly needed when appliqueing leaves.

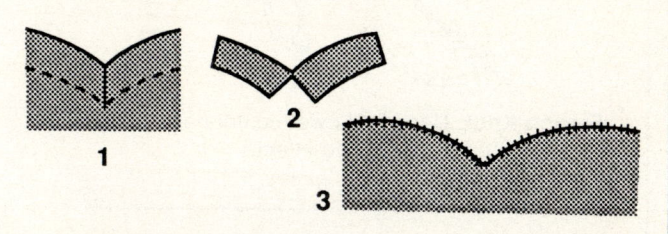

Inside corners: If a sharp dip is part of your shape, such as in the heart design, you will need to clip into the seam allowance to the point. Fold in raw edges to the wrong side. Stitches will need to be done very close together at the indented spot.

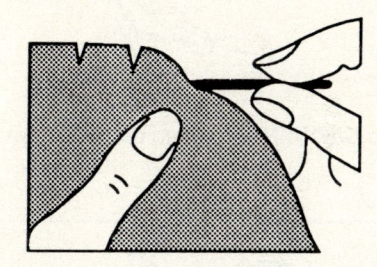

Curved edges: Difficult curved edges are easy to work with if you use your needle to turn the seam allowance underneath as you work.

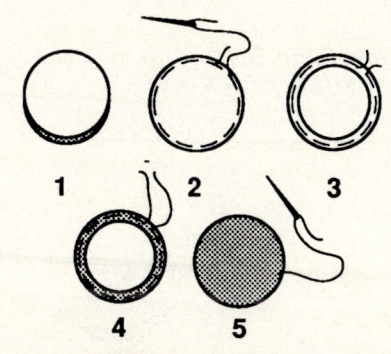

Circles: Cut a cardboard template the size of your finished circle. Sew a basting stitch around fabric piece on seam line. Place fabric piece centered over template and pull basting stitches to gather piece around cardboard shape. Press gently with iron and pull out template. Sew in place.

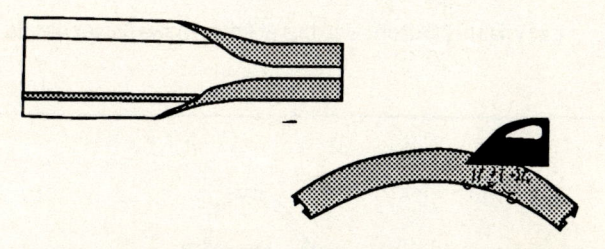

Stems: Stem pieces for flowers and leaves are usually cut on the fabric's bias or diagonal grain. This helps them to curve easily. There are special tools that can help you make your bias strips, or you may purchase premade bias tape. It is not always available in the colors you need. If you have no tools available, you might make a cardboard template in your required finished width and fold your fabric around it and press in place. Press and place on fabric.

Sunbonnet Family Reunion

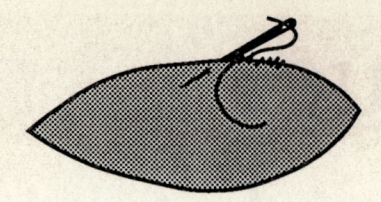

Applique Stitch: Use a close slipstitch or blindstitch to hold your pieces to the background.

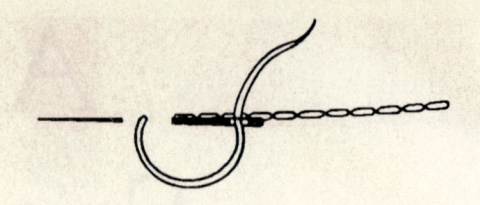

Backstitch: Use for outlining.

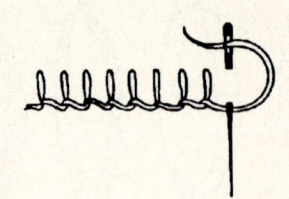

Blanket Stitch: May be used to finish raw edge of applique.

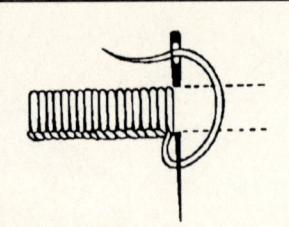

Buttonhole Stitch: Used to finish a raw edge to keep from fraying.

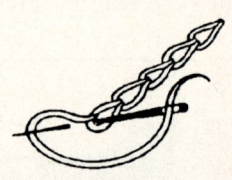

Chain Stitch: Useful when outlining, filling or padding.

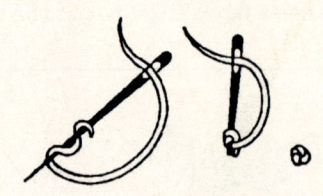

French Knot: Used for flower centers and filling small spaces. Creates a textured effect.

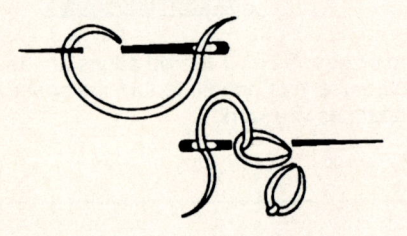

Lazy-Daisy Stitch: Use this stitch to make flower petals.

Long and Short Stitch: Use for shading with several colors or to fill in a large space.

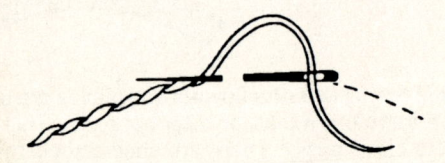

Satin Stitch: A nice stitch to cover small areas. Edges should be neat.

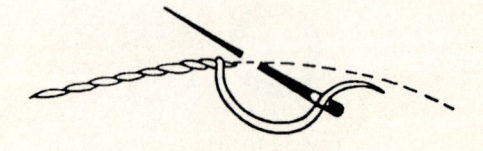

Stem Stitch: Use when a narrow outline is needed.

Oh Glorious Day
Dotty J. Evens • Big Rapids, MI

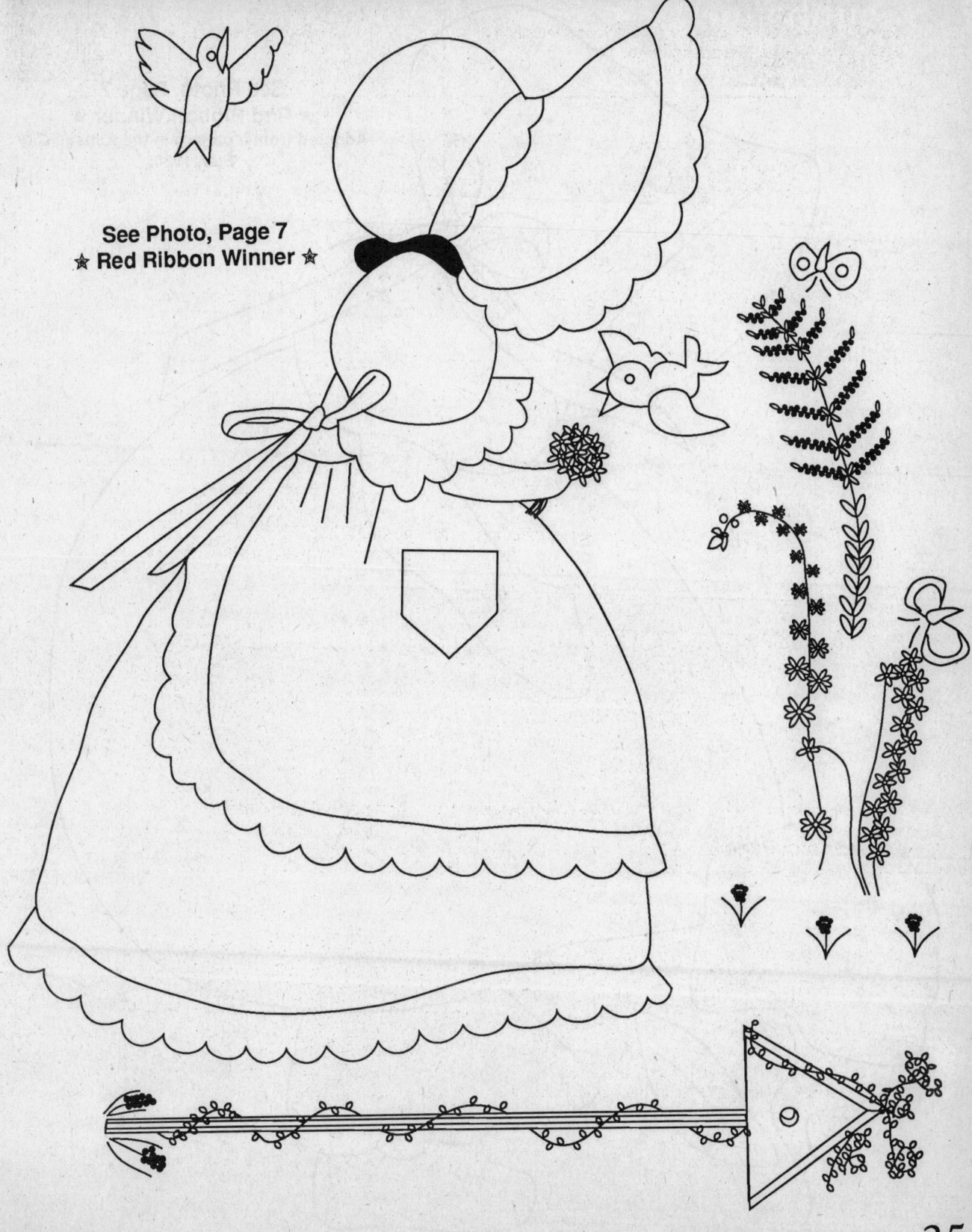

Sunbonnet FAMILY REUNION

See Photo, Page 7
★ Red Ribbon Winner ★

Sunbonnet Family Reunion IV 25

Sunbonnet FAMILY REUNION

Ka Cey Sue
Vera Kaiser • Paola, KS

See Photo, Page 7
✯ **Red Ribbon Winner** ✯
Adapted from a pattern in the *Kansas City Star*, 1930.

26 Sunbonnet Family Reunion IV

Butterfly Run
Violet Conley • New Paris, OH

Sunbonnet FAMILY REUNION

See Photo, Page 7
★ Red Ribbon Winner ★
Adapted from Aunt Martha pattern #3500.

Sunbonnet Family Reunion IV 27

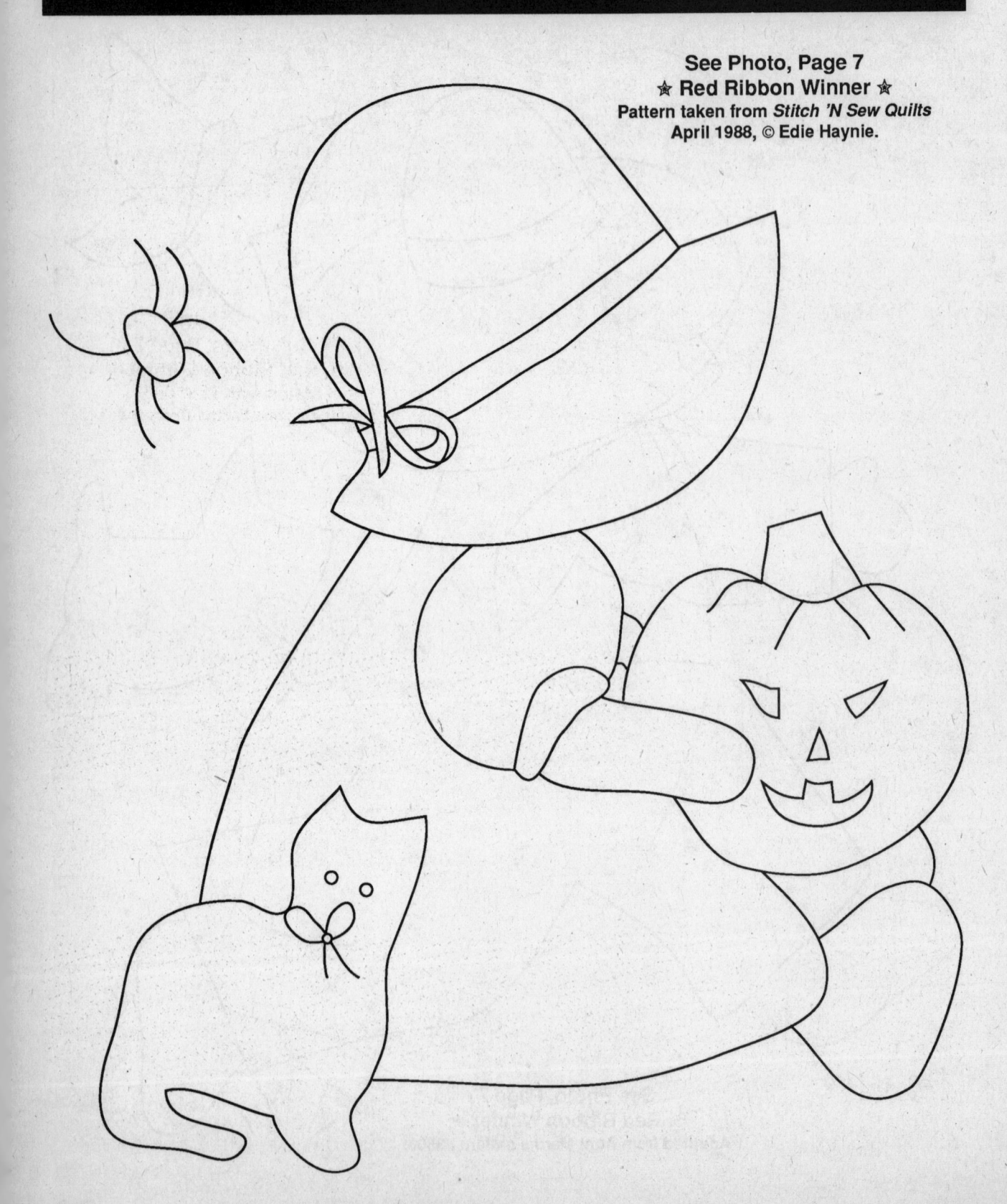

Sunbonnet FAMILY REUNION

It's Fall
Kathryn A. Jones • Marshall, MO

See Photo, Page 7
★ **Red Ribbon Winner** ★
Pattern taken from *Stitch 'N Sew Quilts*
April 1988, © Edie Haynie.

28 Sunbonnet Family Reunion IV

Dancing
Frieda Rippe • Chagrin Falls, OH

Sunbonnet FAMILY REUNION

See Photo, Page 7
✯ Red Ribbon Winner ✯
Match with next page.
Adapted from a Bertha Corbett design.

Sunbonnet Family Reunion IV 29

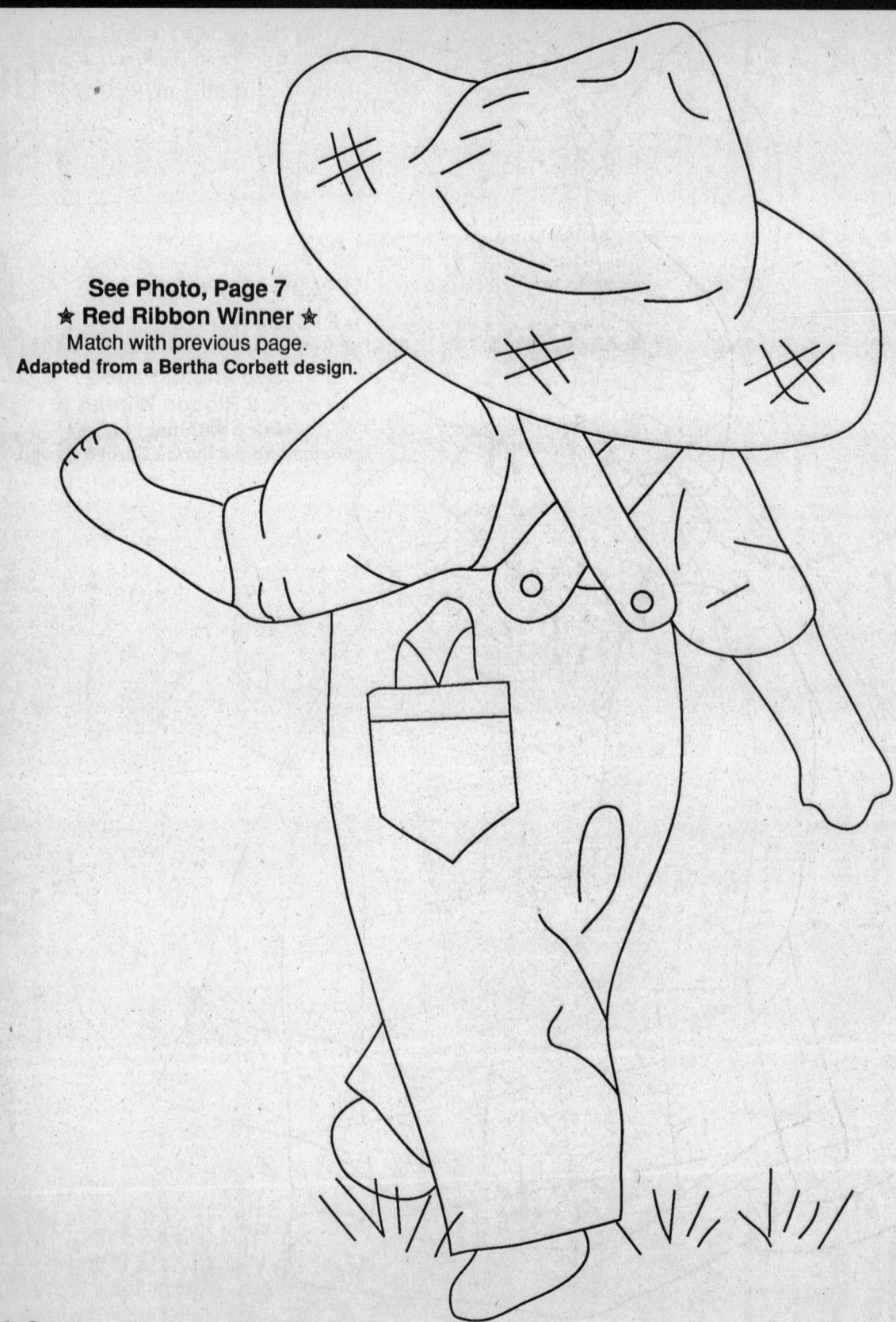

Sunbonnet
FAMILY REUNION

See Photo, Page 7
★ **Red Ribbon Winner** ★
Match with previous page.
Adapted from a Bertha Corbett design.

30 Sunbonnet Family Reunion IV

Sunbonnet Sue & Her Quilt
Karen Searle • Shelley, ID

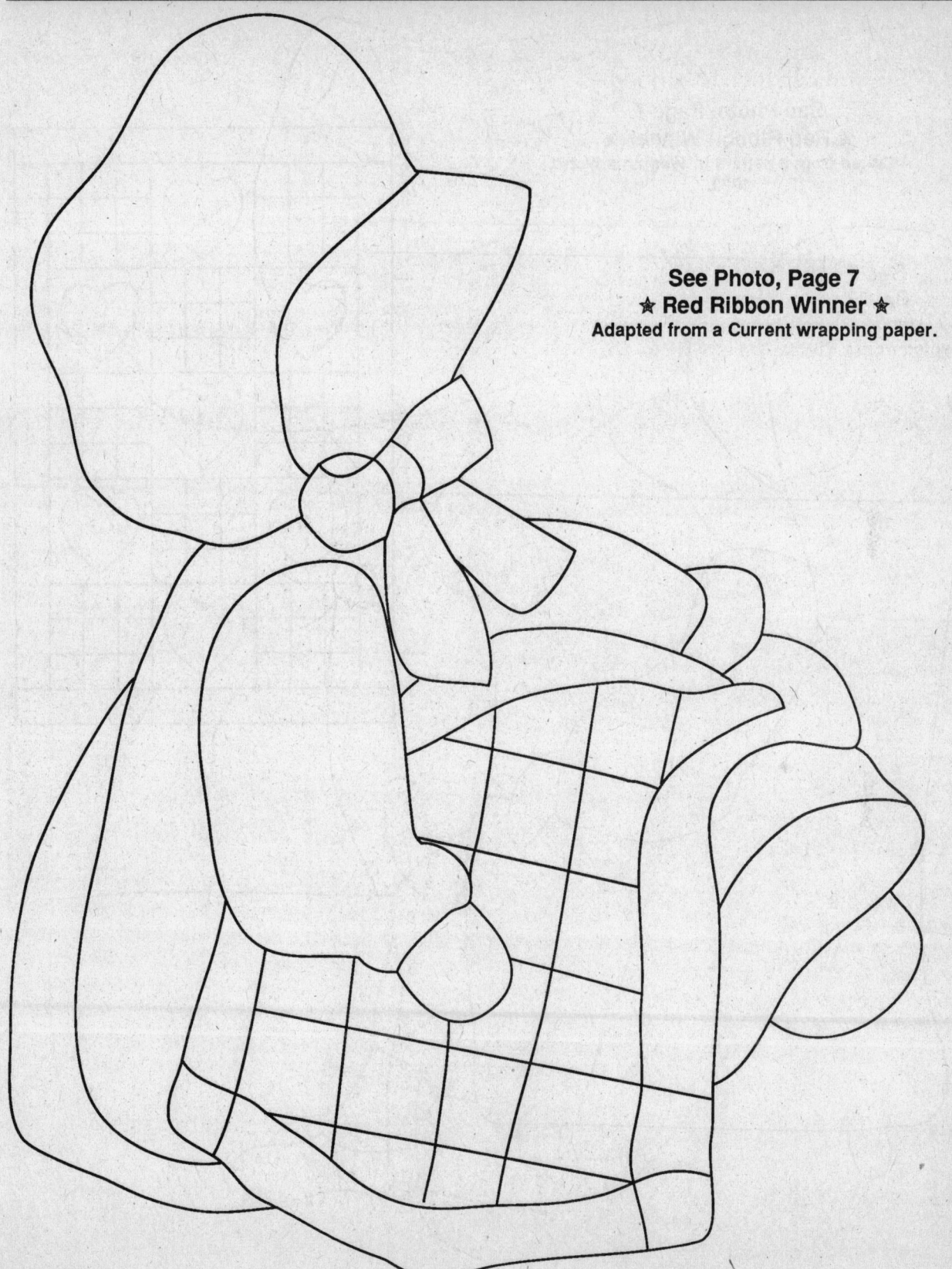

See Photo, Page 7
★ **Red Ribbon Winner** ★
Adapted from a Current wrapping paper.

Sunbonnet Family Reunion IV

Sunbonnet FAMILY REUNION

Lazy Mobcap
Cindy Brown Marquardt • Springfield, MO

See Photo, Page 7
★ **Red Ribbon Winner** ★
Adapted from a pattern in *Woman's World*, 1922.

32 Sunbonnet Family Reunion IV

Colonial Garden Girl
Marian S. Woods • Central City, IA

Sunbonnet FAMILY REUNION

See Photo, Page 7
★ **Red Ribbon Winner** ★
Taken from *The Sunbonnet Family of Quilt Patterns* by Dolores Hinson.

Sunbonnet Family Reunion IV

Sunbonnet FAMILY REUNION

Someday My Quilts Will Come
Patti Connor • Collinsville, IL

See Photo, Page 7
★ **Red Ribbon Winner** ★

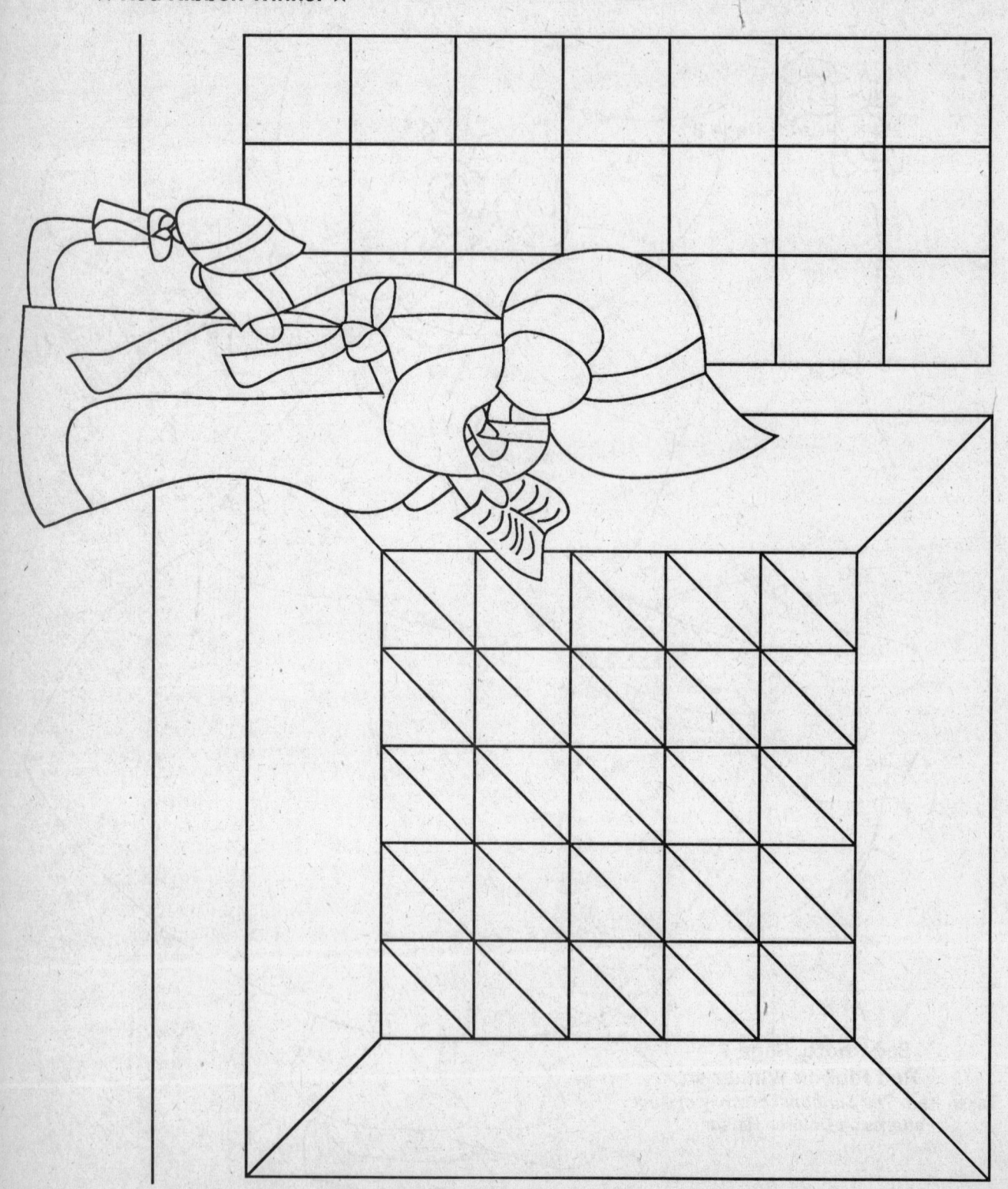

34 Sunbonnet Family Reunion IV

Christmas Is Love
Phyllis Graham • Newport News, VA

Sunbonnet FAMILY REUNION

See Photo, Page 8

Sunbonnet Family Reunion IV 35

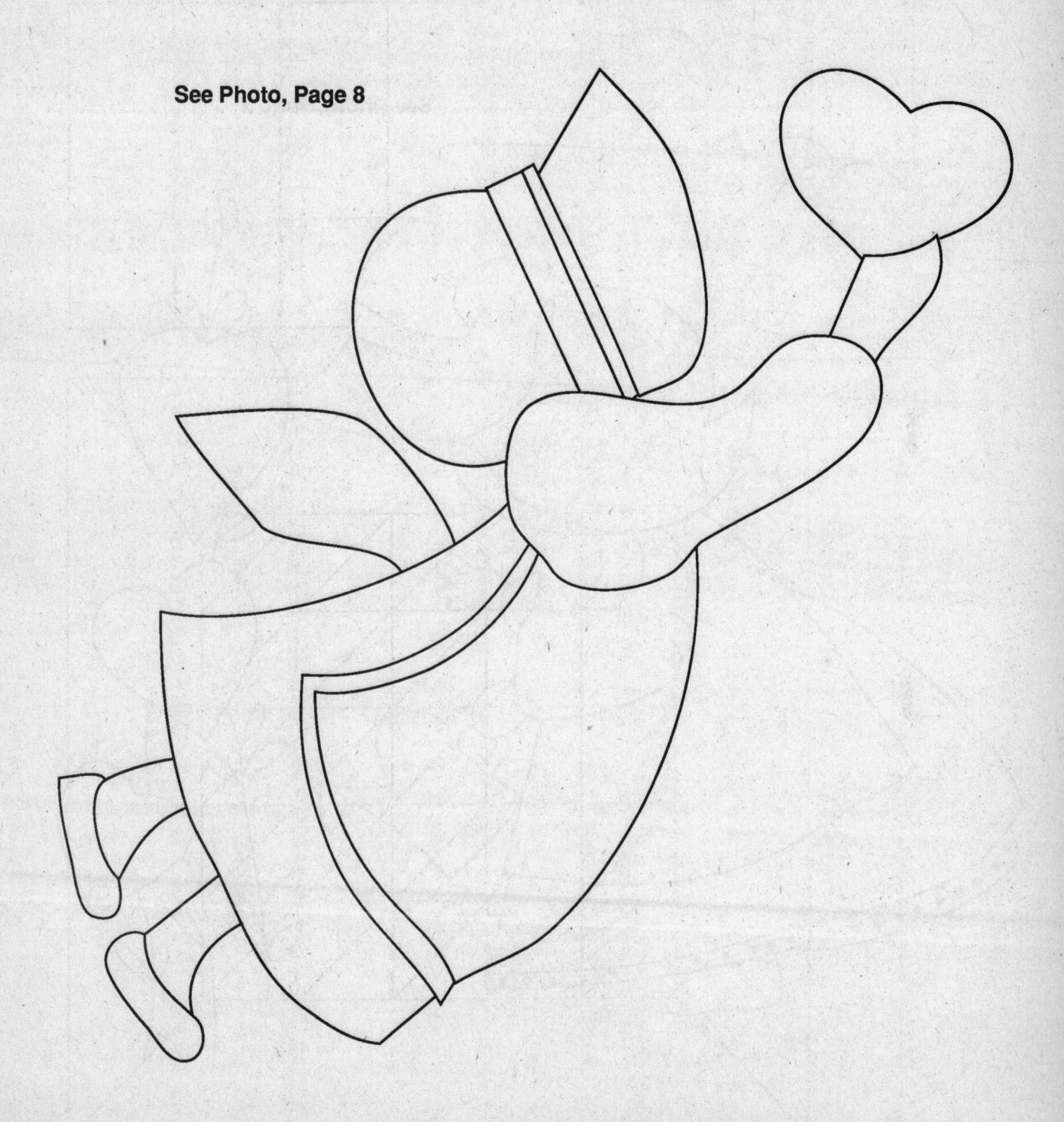

Sunbonnet Sue Loves To Garden
Mary Ann Miller • St. Louis, MO

See Photo, Page 8

36 Sunbonnet Family Reunion IV

I Love Quilts
Twila West • Dimmitt, TX

See Photo, Page 8

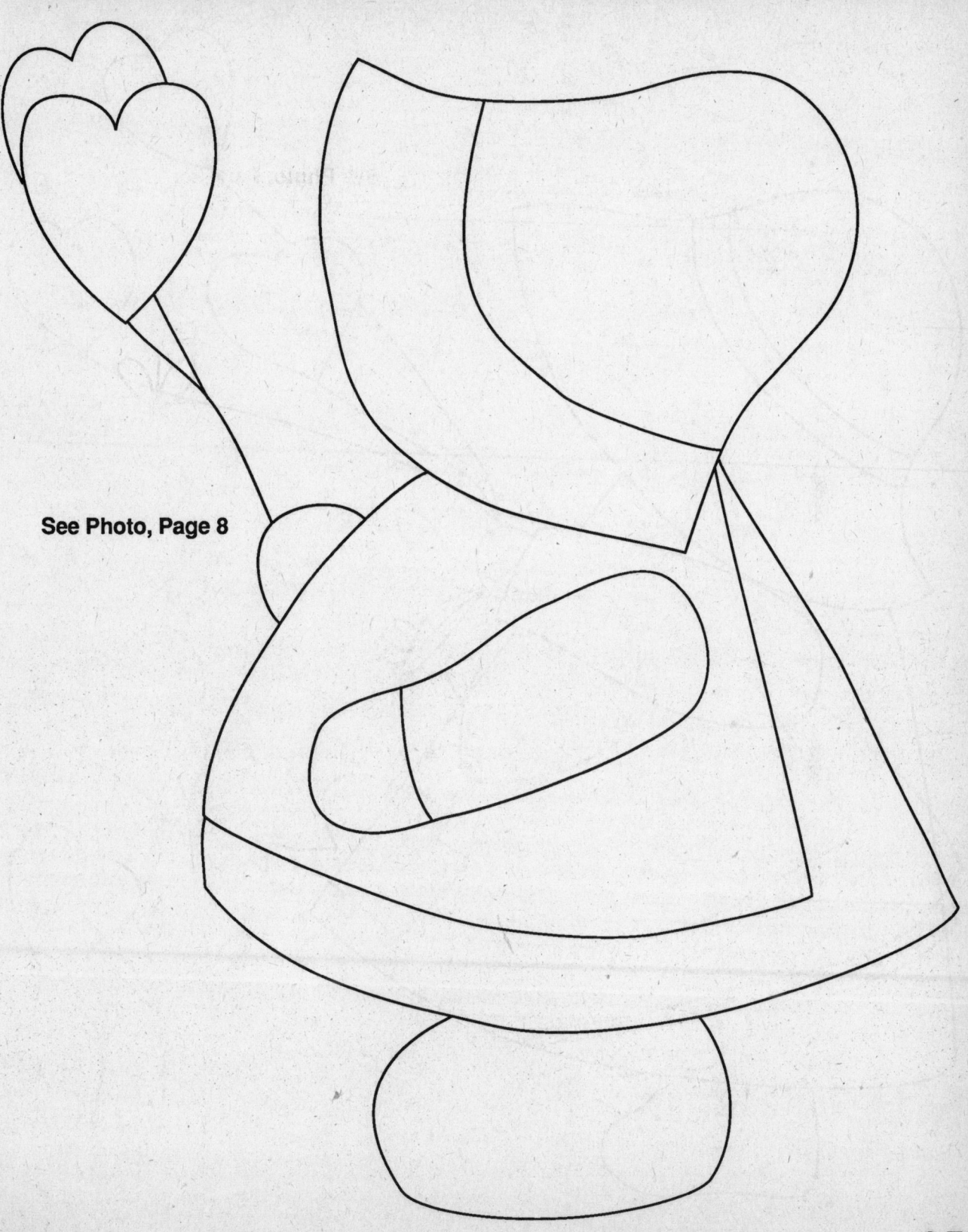

Sunbonnet FAMILY REUNION

All-American Girl
Laura Matkin • San Antonio, TX

All-American Boy
Laura Matkin • San Antonio, TX

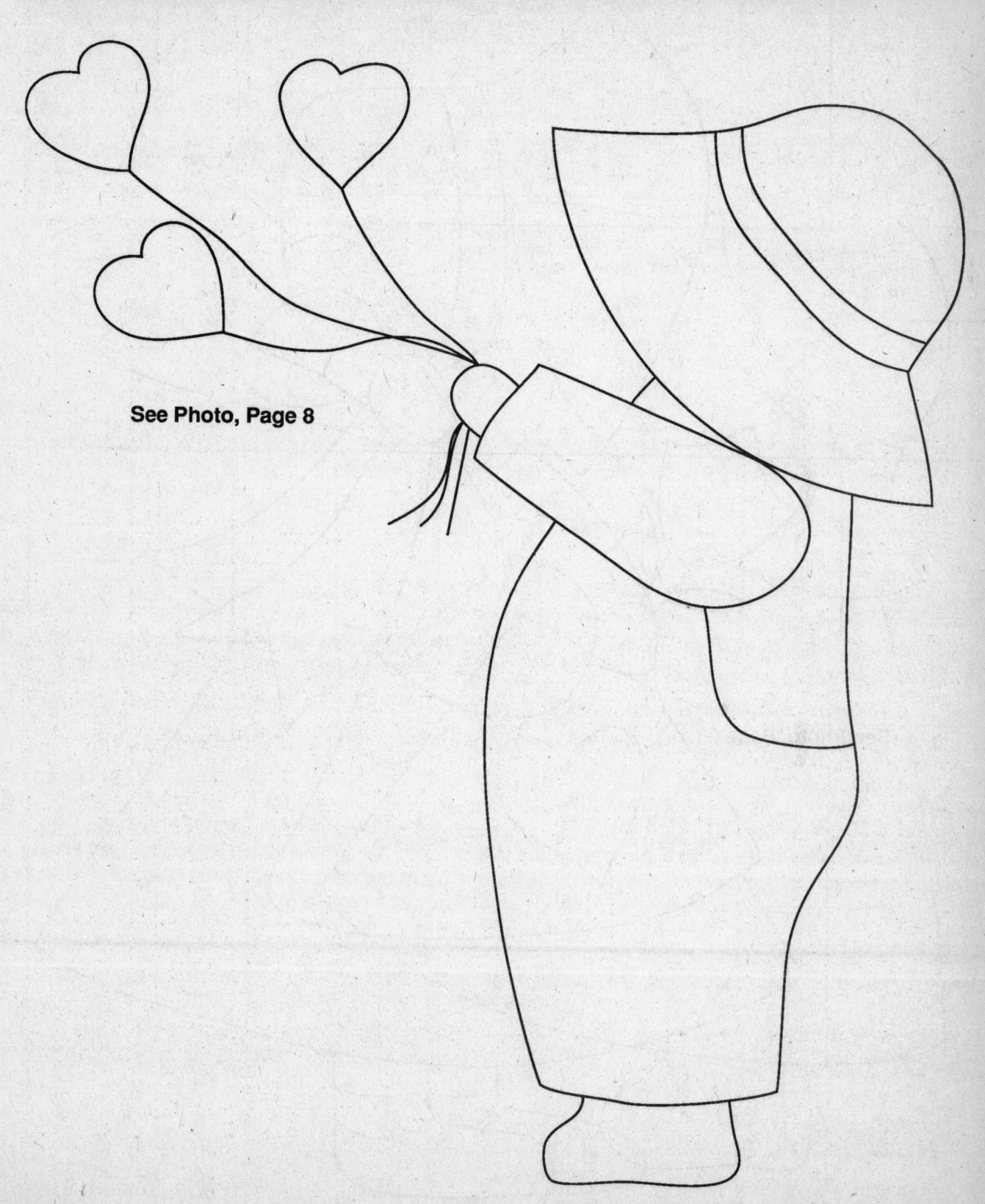

Sunbonnet FAMILY REUNION

See Photo, Page 8

Sunbonnet Family Reunion IV 39

Sunbonnet FAMILY REUNION

Spring Flower
Brenda Dodd • Noble, OK

See Photo, Page 8

Brown-Eyed Susan
Eileen Squitiro • New Milton, WV

See Photo, Page 8

Sunbonnet FAMILY REUNION

I'll Give My Heart To You
Margaret McClellan • Osawatomie, KS

See Photo, Page 8

42 Sunbonnet Family Reunion IV

Pink Lace
Tina Boyd • Live Oak, FL

Sunbonnet FAMILY REUNION

See Photo, Page 8

Sunbonnet Family Reunion IV 43

Sunbonnet FAMILY REUNION

My Patchwork Kitty
Lynda G. Boucke • St. Petersburg, FL

See Photo, Page 9
Adapted from *Country Children* by Pat Cox.

44 Sunbonnet Family Reunion IV

Two Friends
Carol January • S. Weymouth, MA

Sunbonnet FAMILY REUNION

See Photo, Page 9

Sunbonnet Family Reunion IV 45

Sunbonnet FAMILY REUNION

Ellie & Emma Out For A Walk
Eleanor Wright • Santa Barbara, CA

See Photo, Page 9

46 Sunbonnet Family Reunion IV

Here Kitty, Kitty
Gail M. Hodge • Garden City, MI

Sunbonnet FAMILY REUNION

See Photo, Page 9

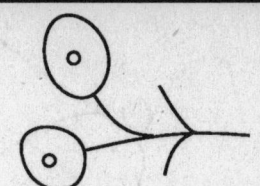

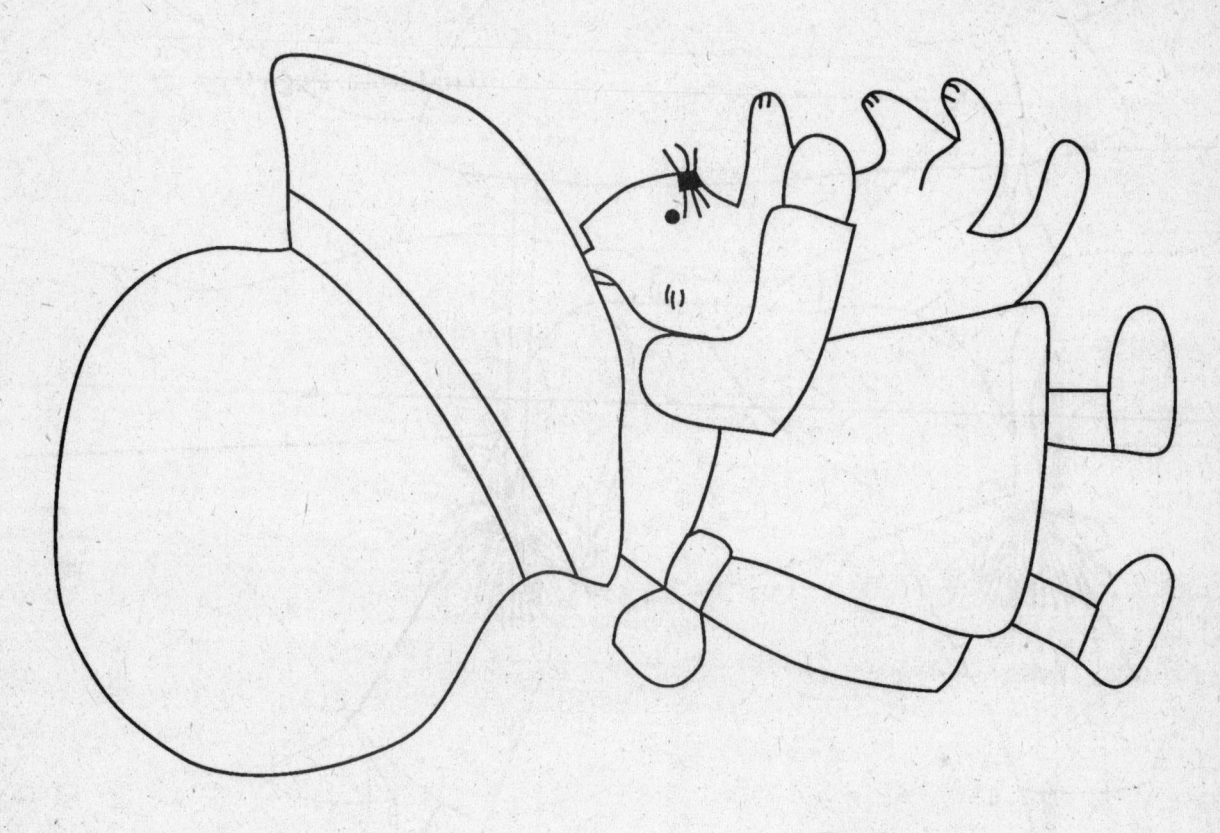

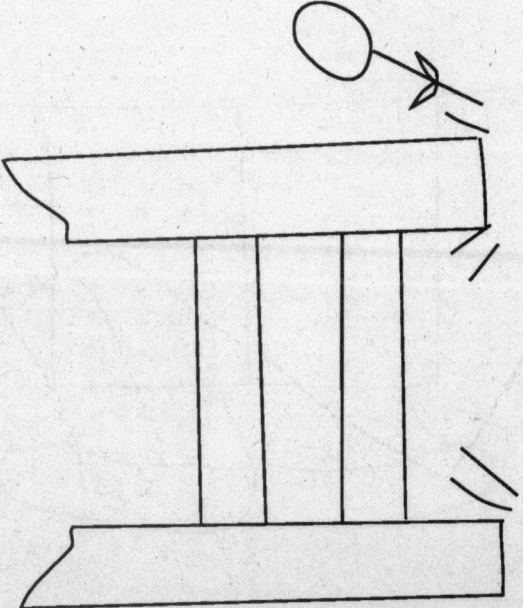

Sunbonnet Family Reunion IV 47

Sunbonnet FAMILY REUNION

Tempura Sue & Kitty Wong
Linda Riedi • DePere, WI

See Photo, Page 9

48 Sunbonnet Family Reunion IV

Flying A Balloon
Elrid Johnson • Brookfield, WI

Sunbonnet FAMILY REUNION

See Photo, Page 9

Sunbonnet Family Reunion IV

Sunbonnet Girl Walks Her Dog
Barbara J. Heaton • Park Forest, IL

See Photo, Page 9

50 Sunbonnet Family Reunion IV

Now You Have It, Kitty
Jane Talso • Albuquerque, NM

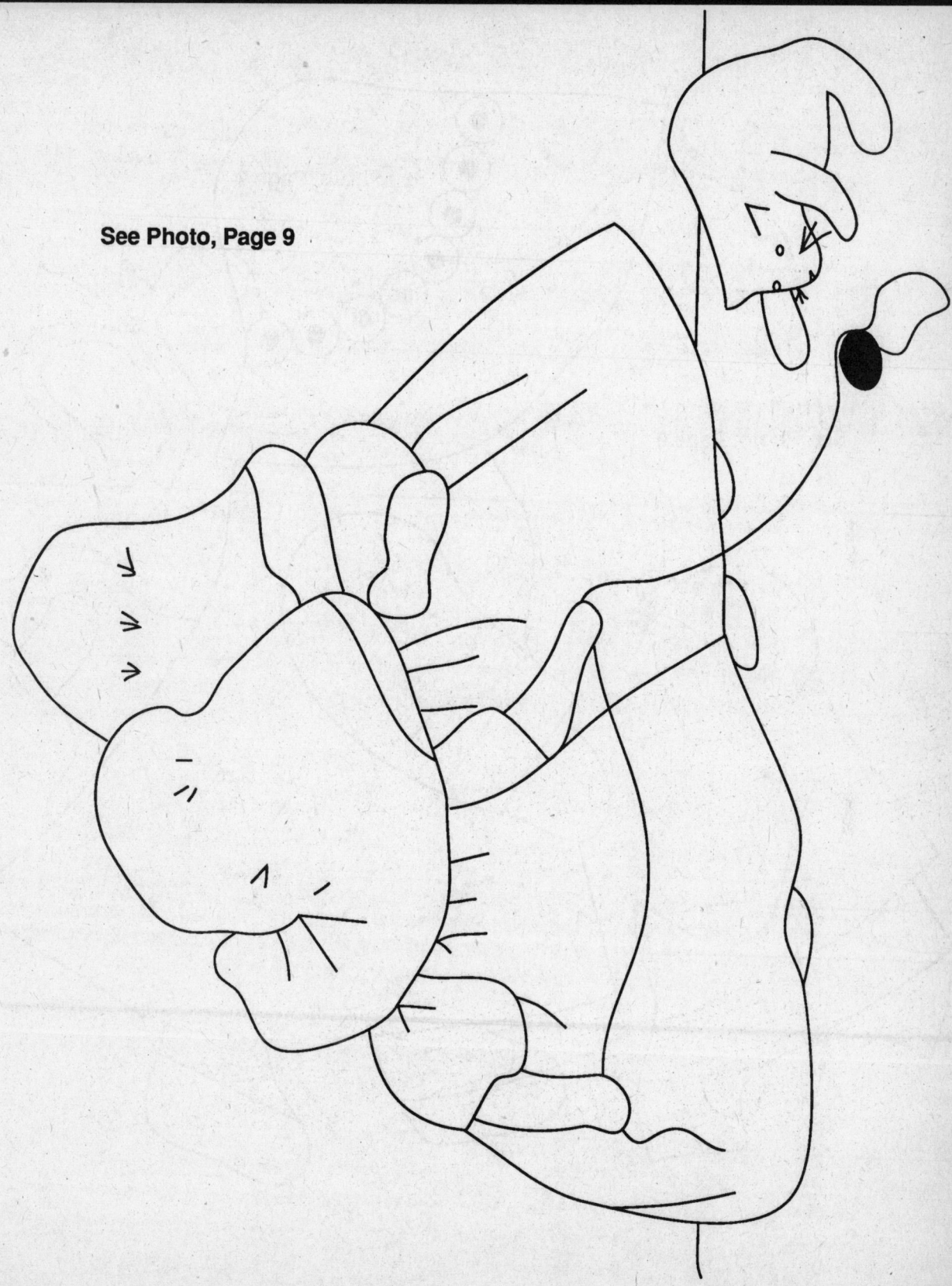

Sunbonnet FAMILY REUNION

See Photo, Page 9

Sunbonnet Family Reunion IV 51

Sunbonnet FAMILY REUNION

A 1920s Pair
Betty Goodwin • Camp Hill, PA

See Photo, Page 9

52 Sunbonnet Family Reunion IV

On Her Way
Carol A. Miller • Mount Olive, IL

Sunbonnet FAMILY REUNION

See Photo, Page 10
Match with next page.

Sunbonnet Family Reunion IV

Sunbonnet
FAMILY REUNION

See Photo, Page 10
Match with previous page.

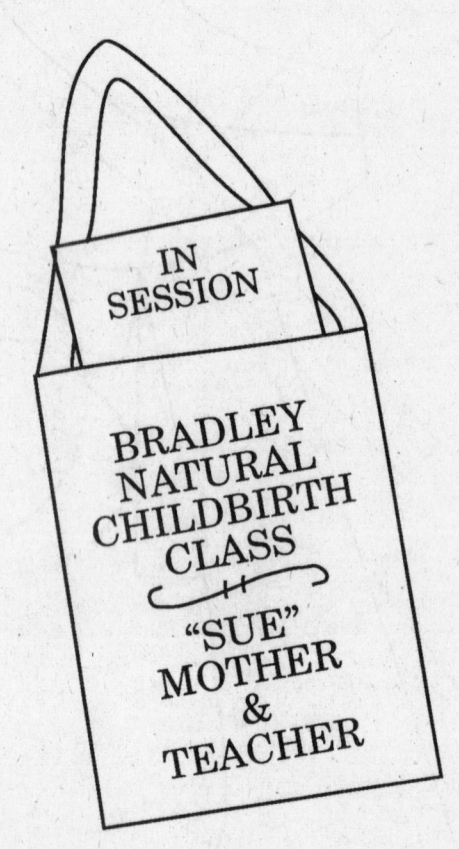

IN SESSION

BRADLEY
NATURAL
CHILDBIRTH
CLASS

"SUE"
MOTHER
&
TEACHER

Sunbonnet Family Reunion IV

Sunbonnet Sue Graduates
I.V. Crawford • Tyler, TX

See Photo, Page 10

Sunbonnet Family Reunion IV 55

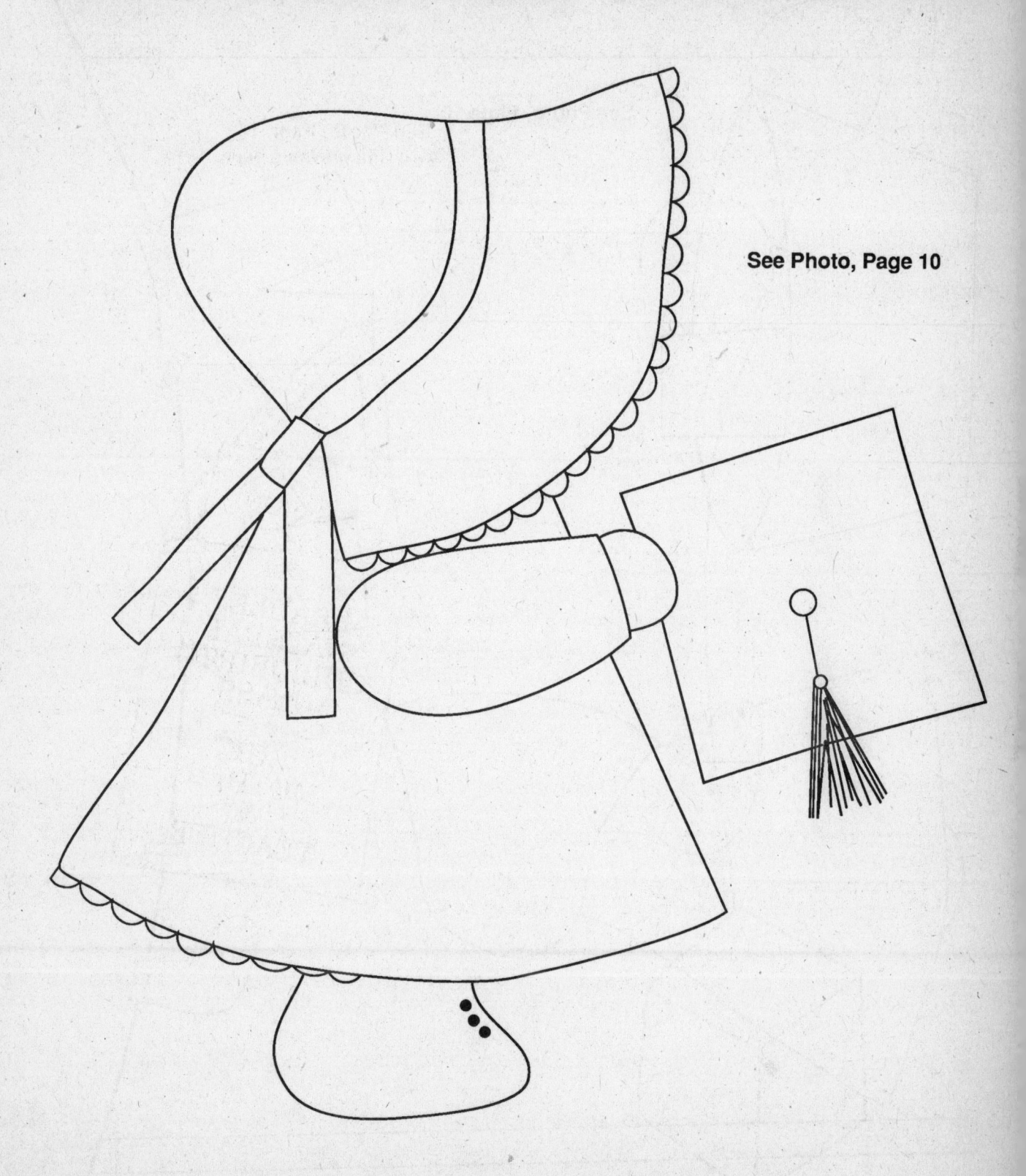

Sunbonnet FAMILY REUNION — This Is The Way We Wash Our Clothes
Jo Barbera • Flemington, NJ

See Photo, Page 10

56 Sunbonnet Family Reunion IV

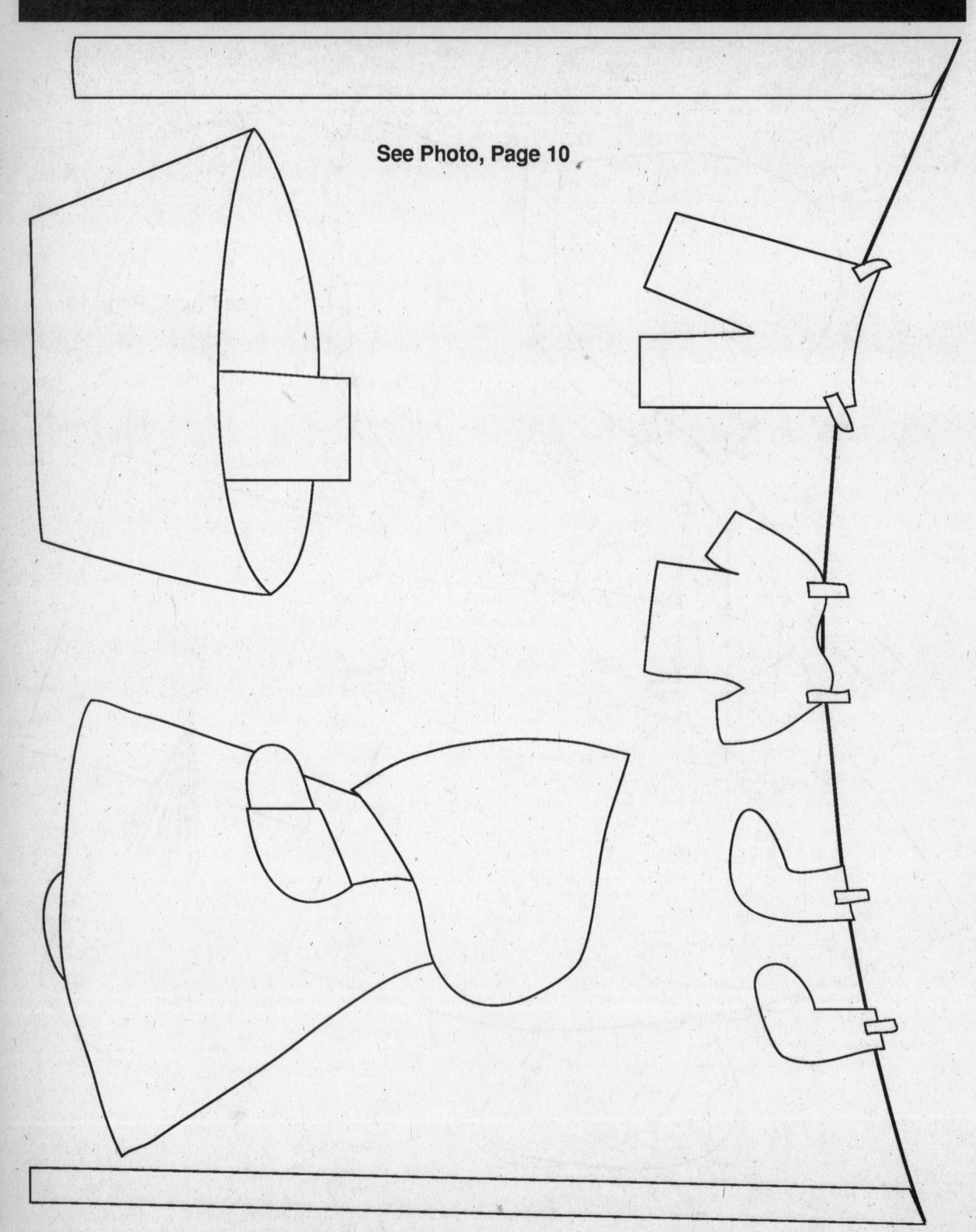

Maiden On A Swing
Shari Schmidt • Turpin, OK

Sunbonnet FAMILY REUNION

See Photo, Page 10

Sunbonnet Family Reunion IV 57

Sunbonnet FAMILY REUNION

June Bride
Pat Pierson • Mechanicsburg, PA

See Photo, Page 10
Taken from *Stitch 'N Sew Quilts* April 1988, © Edie Haynie.

58 Sunbonnet Family Reunion IV

Sunbonnet Girl With Balloon
Ethel B. Kidwell • Kansas City, MO

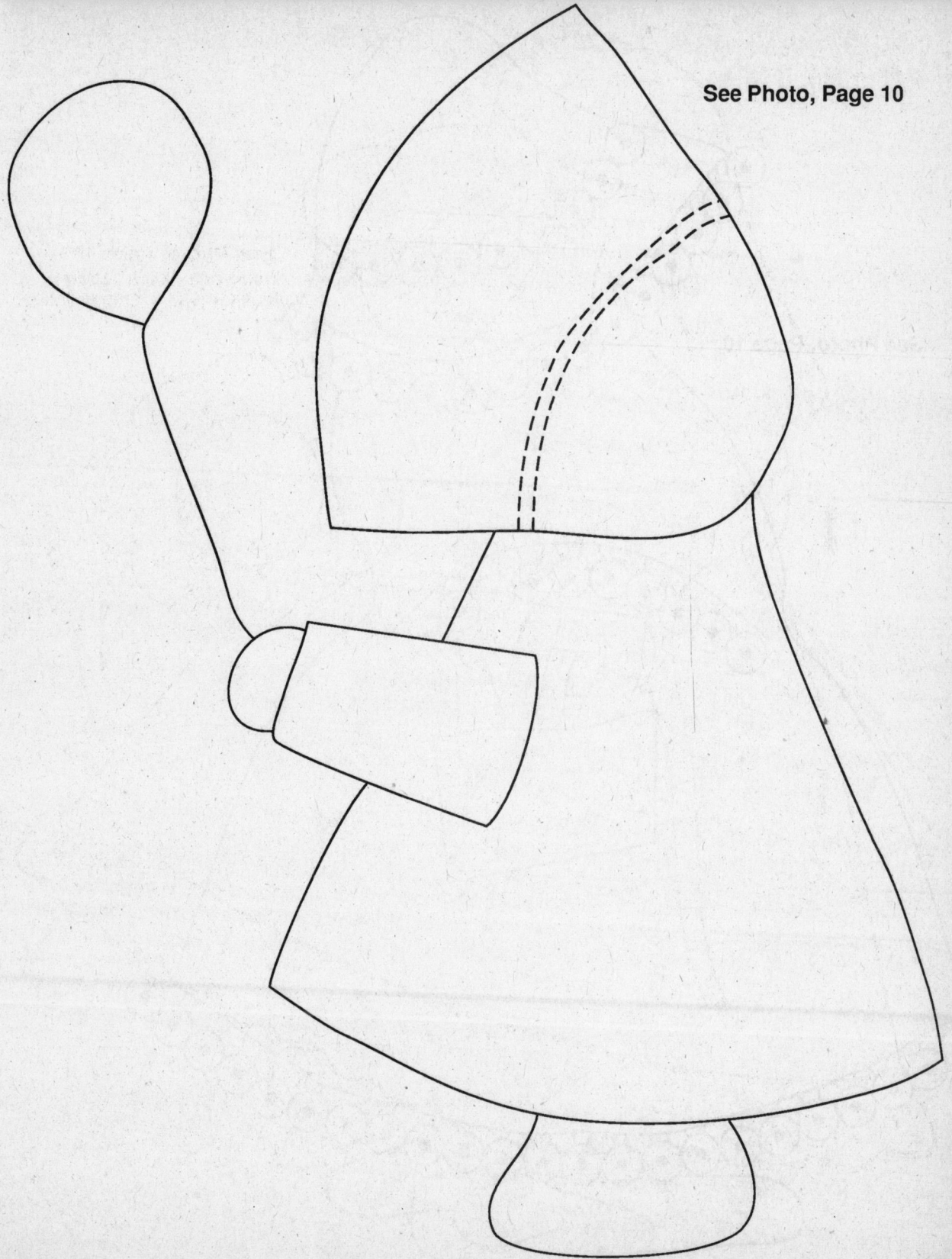

See Photo, Page 10

Sunbonnet Family Reunion IV 59

Sunbonnet FAMILY REUNION

Going Shopping For Quilts
Ione Trapp • N. Vernon, IN

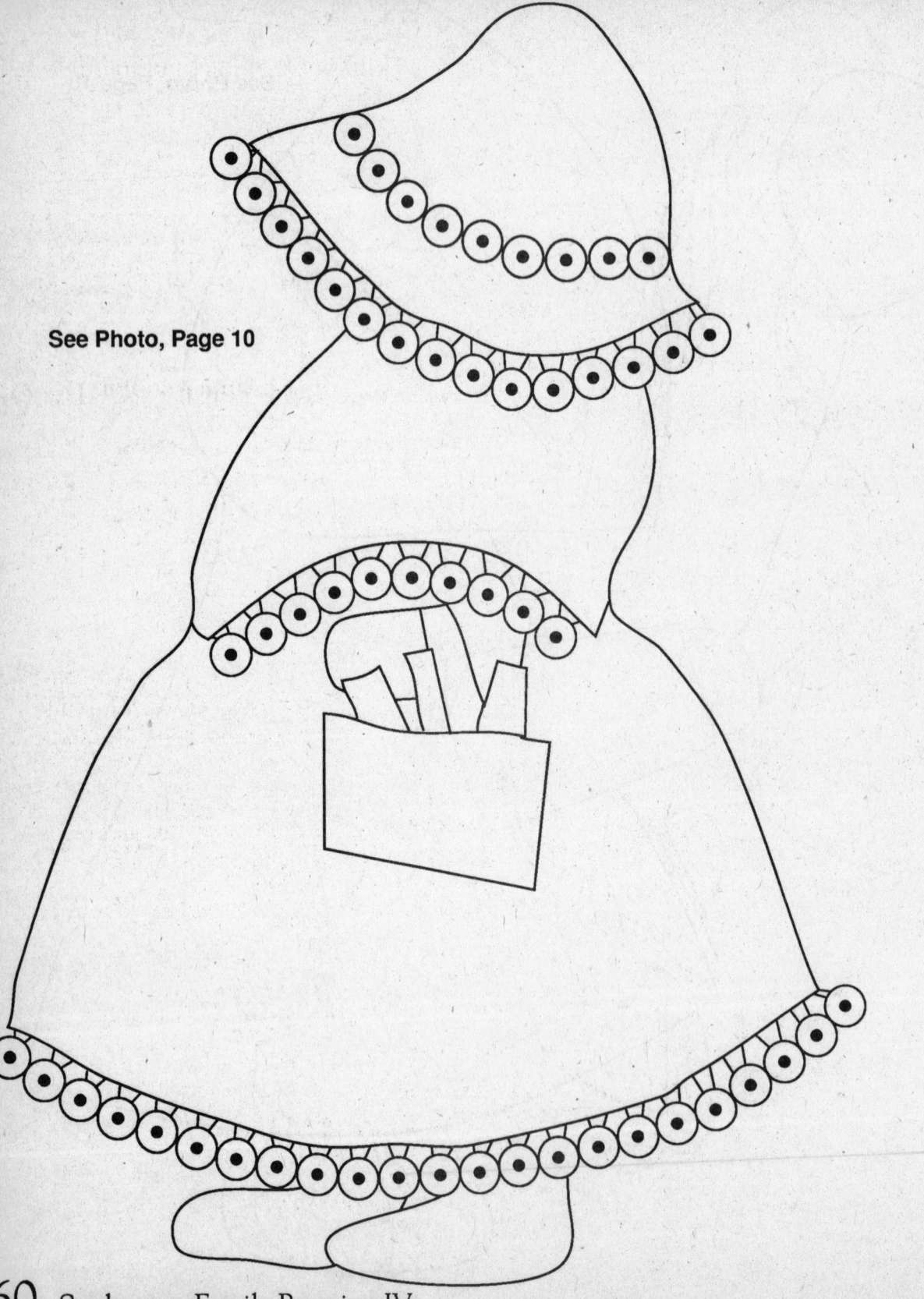

See Photo, Page 10

60 Sunbonnet Family Reunion IV

Ring Around A Posy
Alta M. Parrish • Carmel, IN

Sunbonnet FAMILY REUNION

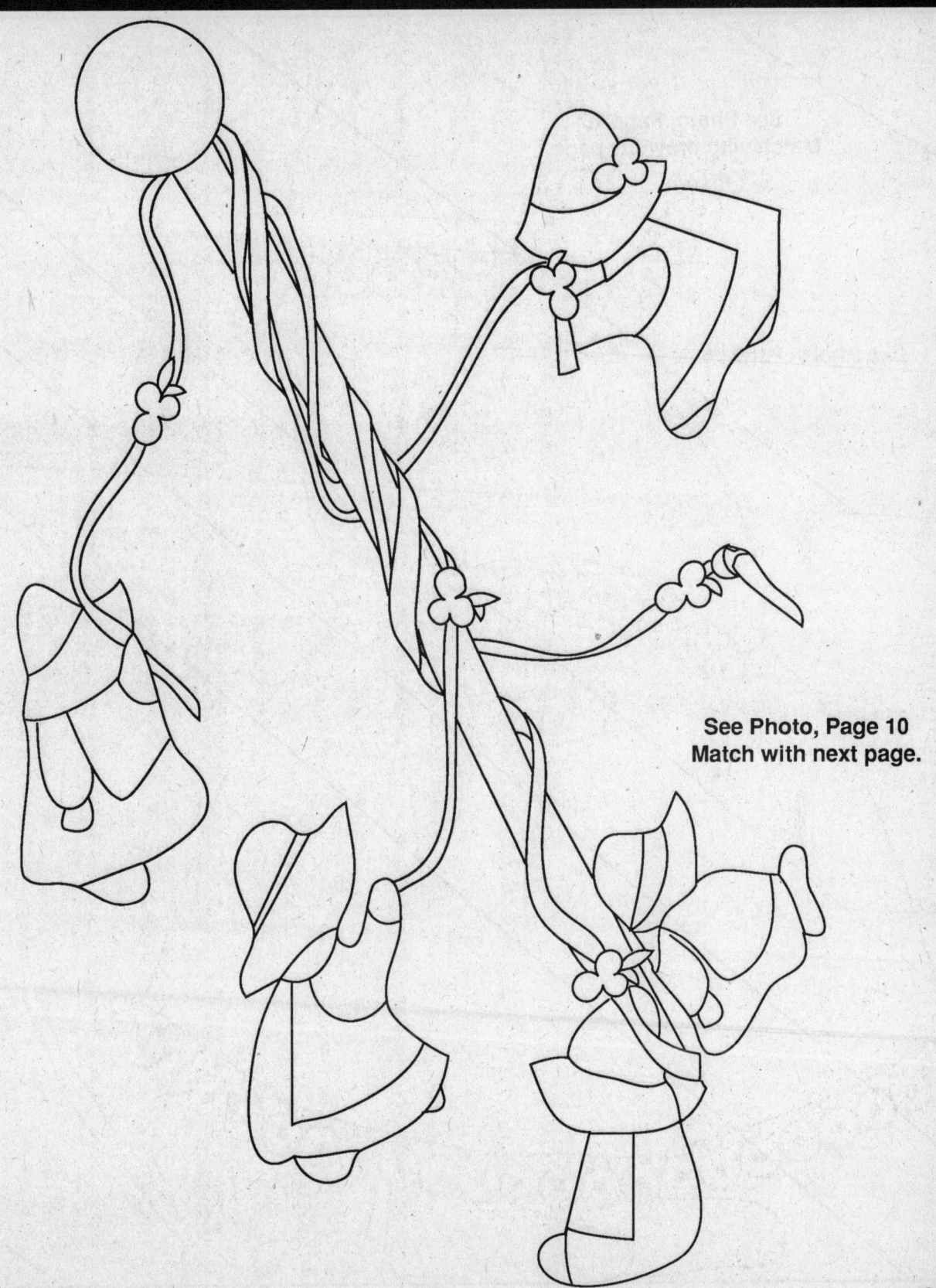

See Photo, Page 10
Match with next page.

Sunbonnet Family Reunion IV 61

See Photo, Page 10
Match with previous page.

62 Sunbonnet Family Reunion IV

Sunbonnet Sue Uses The Curling Iron
Pat Vodry • Big Rapids, MI

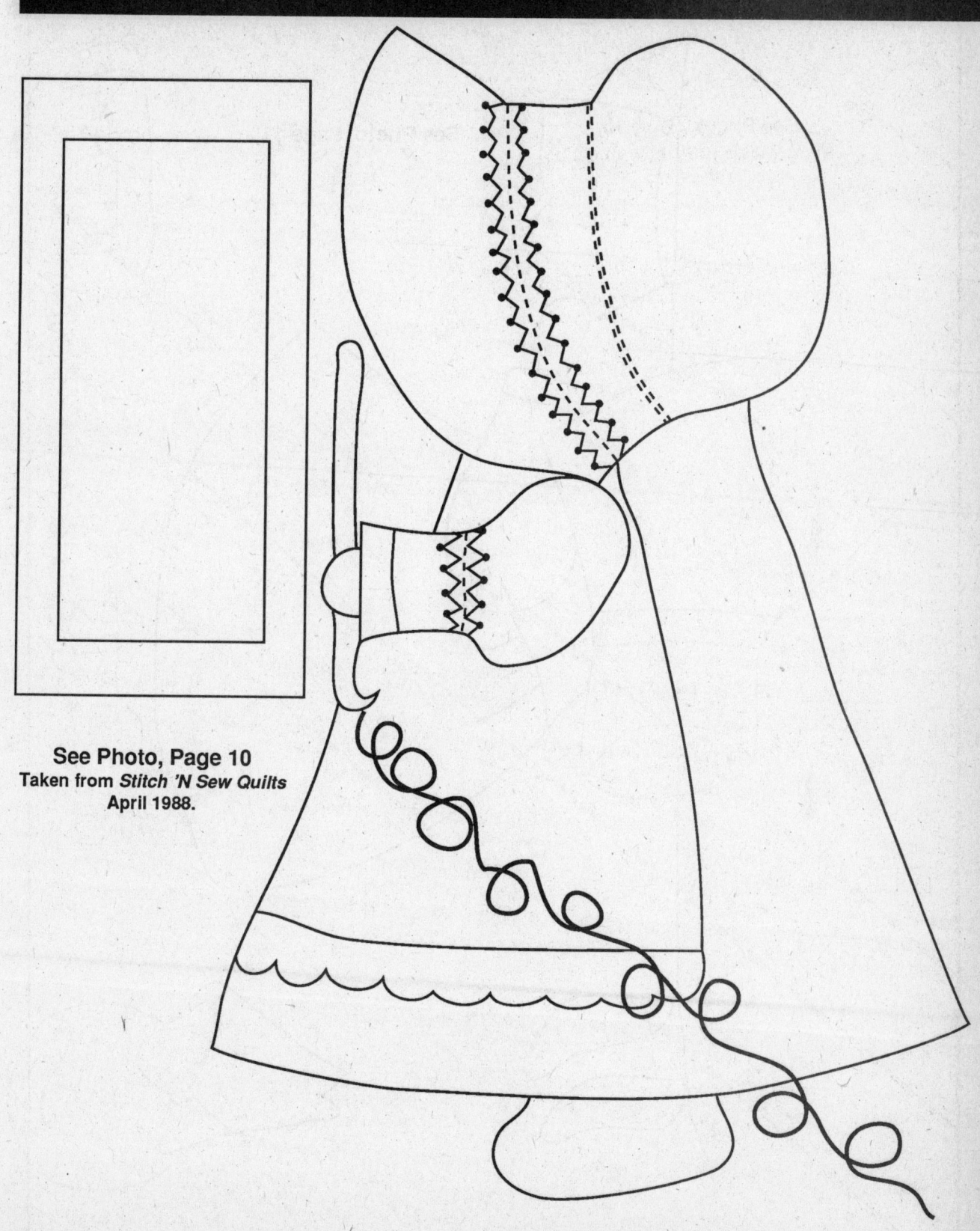

Sunbonnet FAMILY REUNION

See Photo, Page 10
Taken from *Stitch 'N Sew Quilts* April 1988.

Sunbonnet Family Reunion IV 63

Sunbonnet Wash Day
Patti Martinez • Harvard, IL

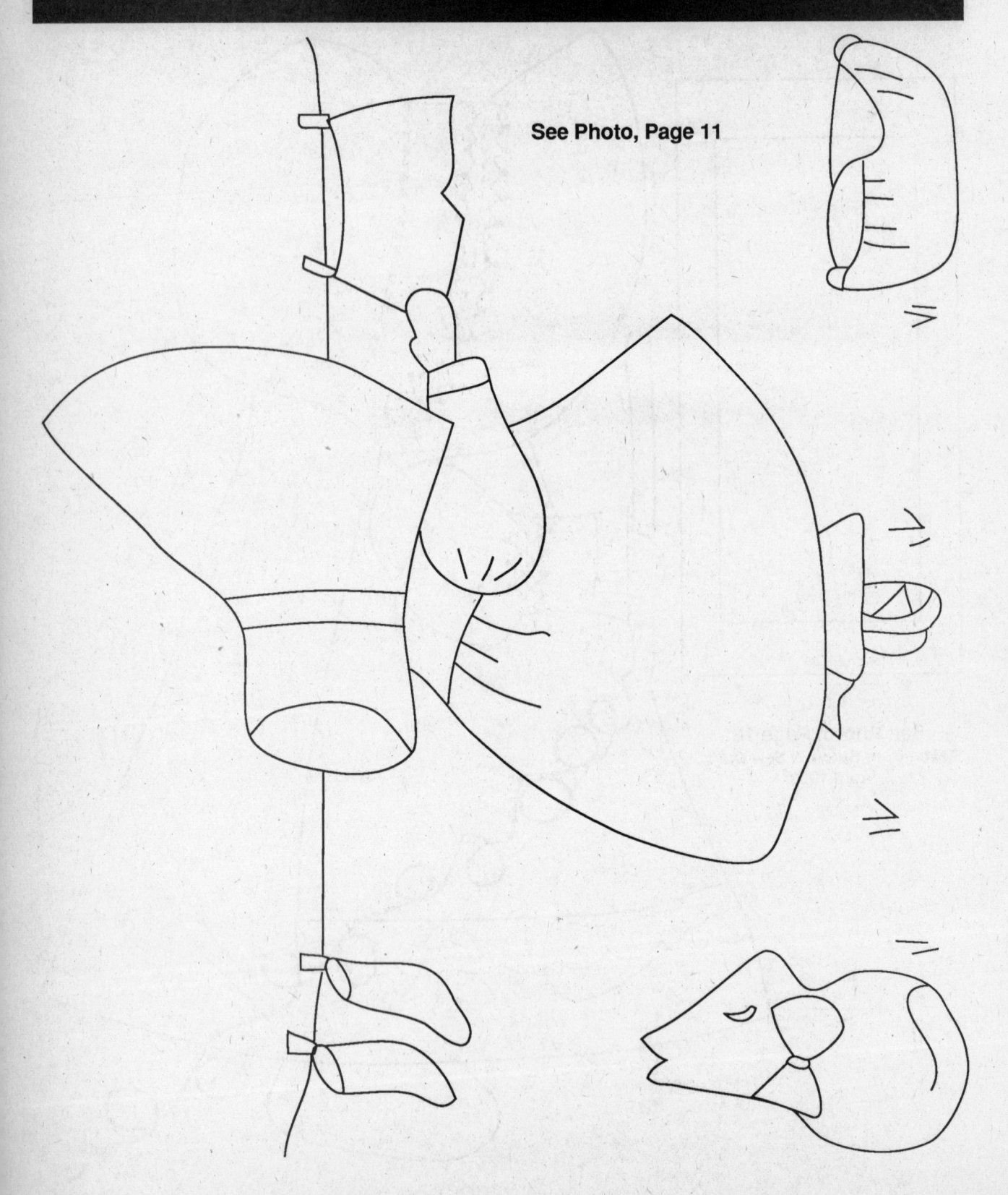

See Photo, Page 11

Salmon Drying Alaska
Fae DeWitt • Hoonah, AK

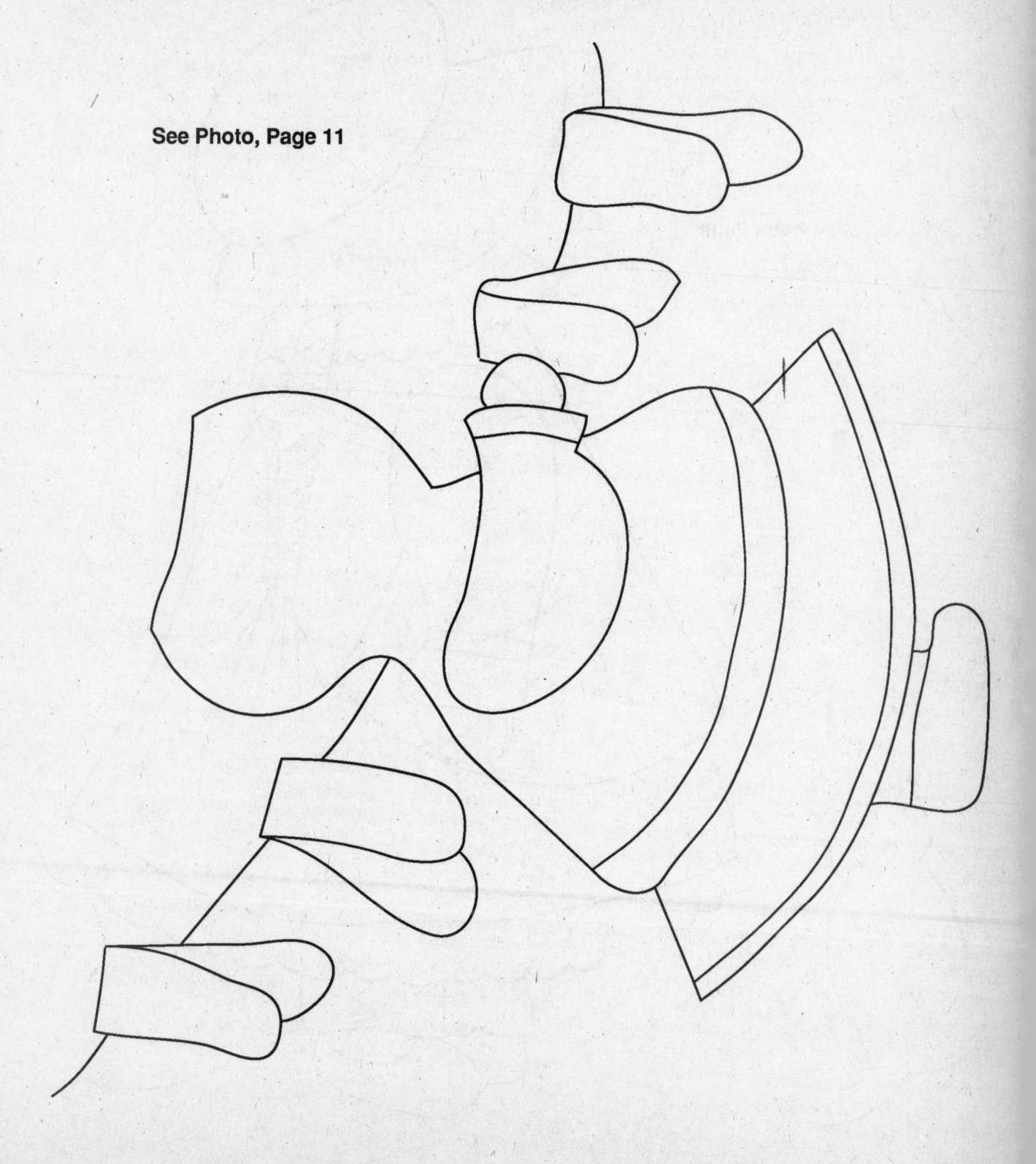

See Photo, Page 11

Sunbonnet Family Reunion IV

Sunbonnet FAMILY REUNION

Priscilla & Kitty
Francis Pinkerton • Littlefield, TX

See Photo, Page 11

66 Sunbonnet Family Reunion IV

Fishing Boy
Teresa M. Heinze • Rolla, MO

See Photo, Page 11

Sunbonnet Family Reunion IV 67

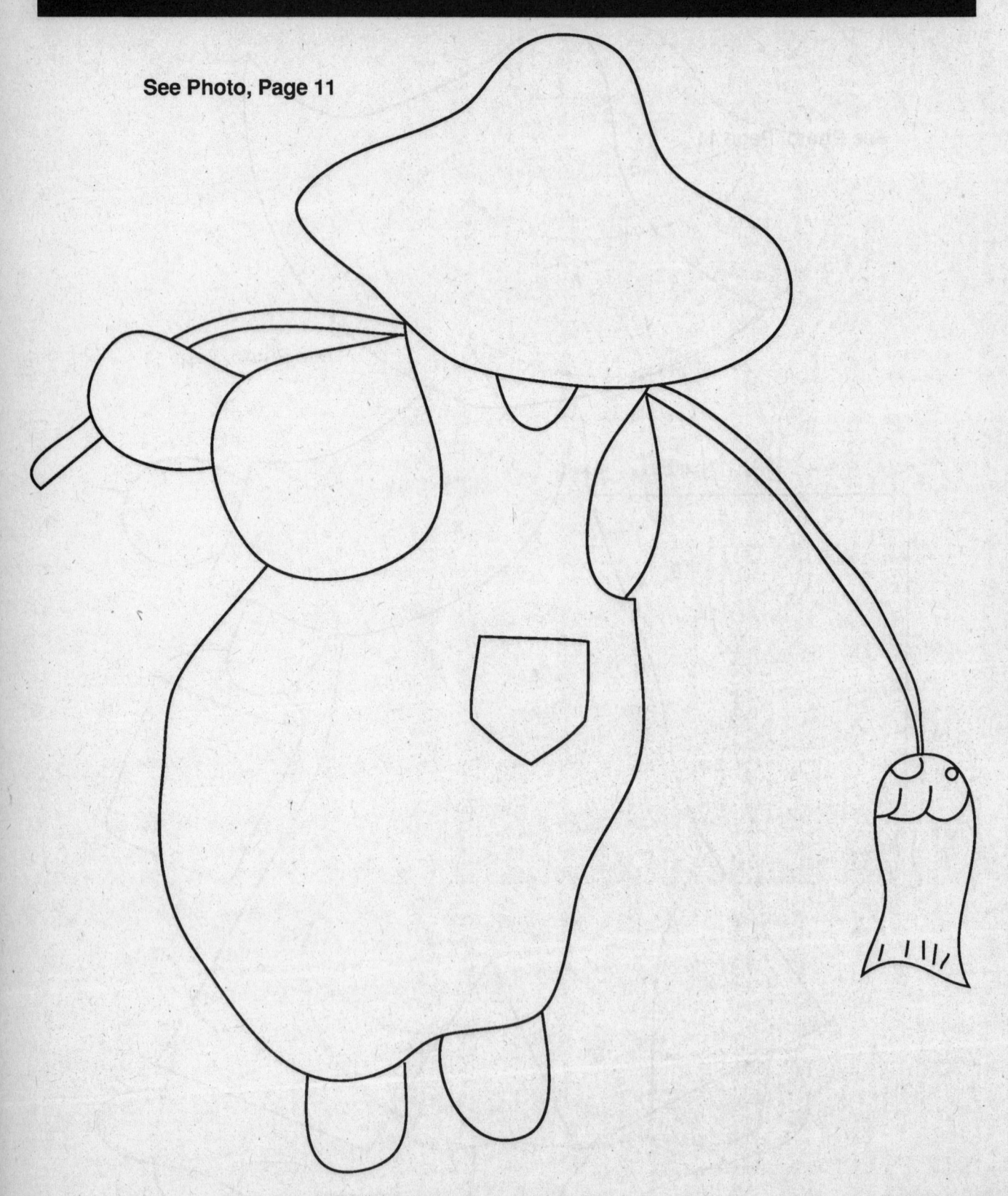

Sunbonnet FAMILY REUNION

Gone Fishing
Marie M. Kelly • Hemet, CA

See Photo, Page 11

68 Sunbonnet Family Reunion IV

Strawhat Sam & Patches
Sallie Townsend • Westland, MI

Sunbonnet FAMILY REUNION

See Photo, Page 11

Sunbonnet Family Reunion IV

Sunbonnet FAMILY REUNION

Bicycle Becky
Jeanette B. Doerr • Rochester, NY

See Photo, Page 11

70 Sunbonnet Family Reunion IV

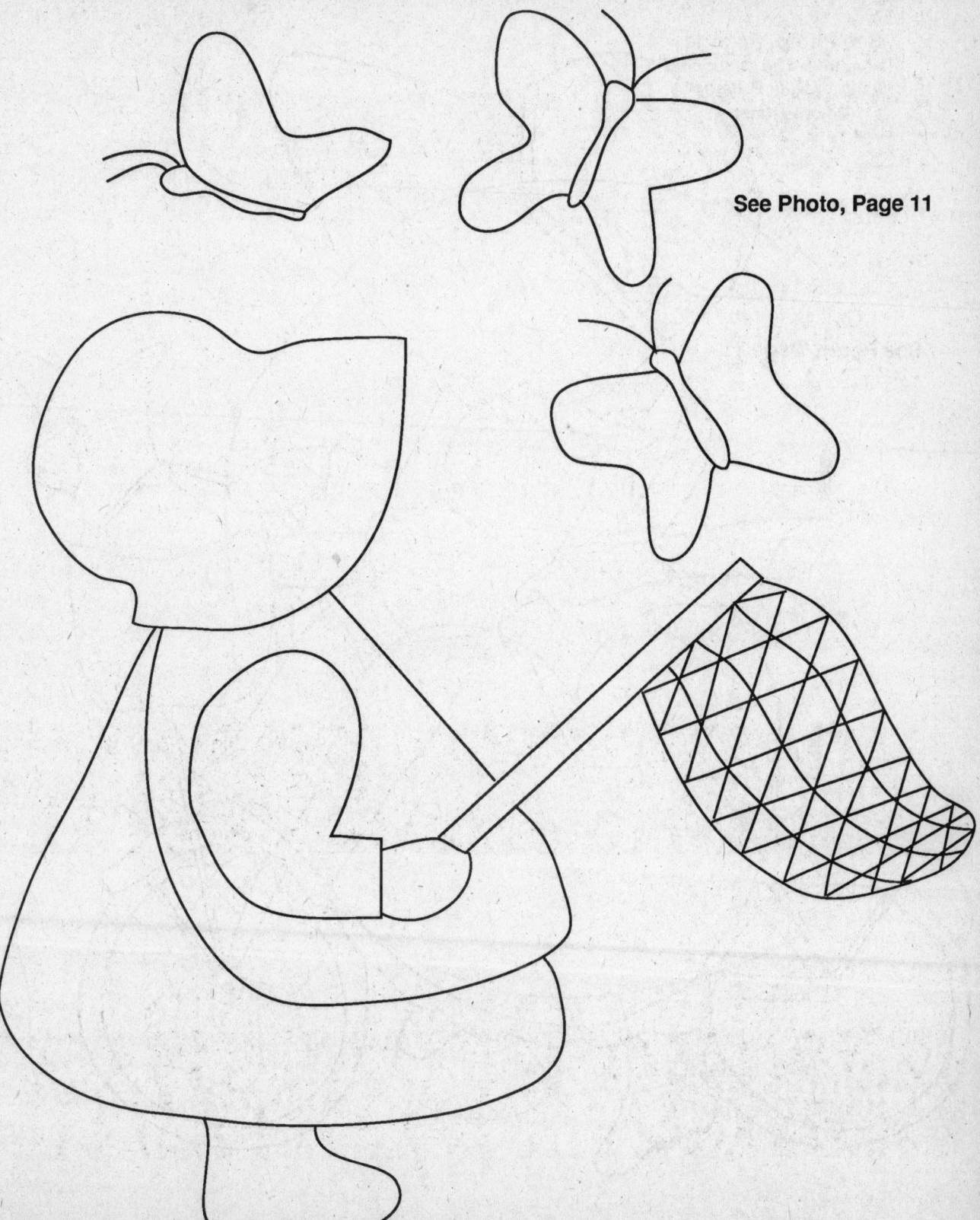

Flutterbys
Janie Mountain Baker • Panorama City, CA

Sunbonnet FAMILY REUNION

See Photo, Page 11

Sunbonnet Family Reunion IV 71

Sunbonnet FAMILY REUNION

Umbrella Sue
Eloise Lewis McCartney • Poland, OH

See Photo, Page 11
Taken from *The Sunbonnet Family of Quilt Patterns* by Dolores Hinson.

72 Sunbonnet Family Reunion IV

Sunbonnet Girl (1934)
Ruby Rupert • Adrian, MI

Sunbonnet FAMILY REUNION

See Photo, Page 12

Sunbonnet Family Reunion IV 73

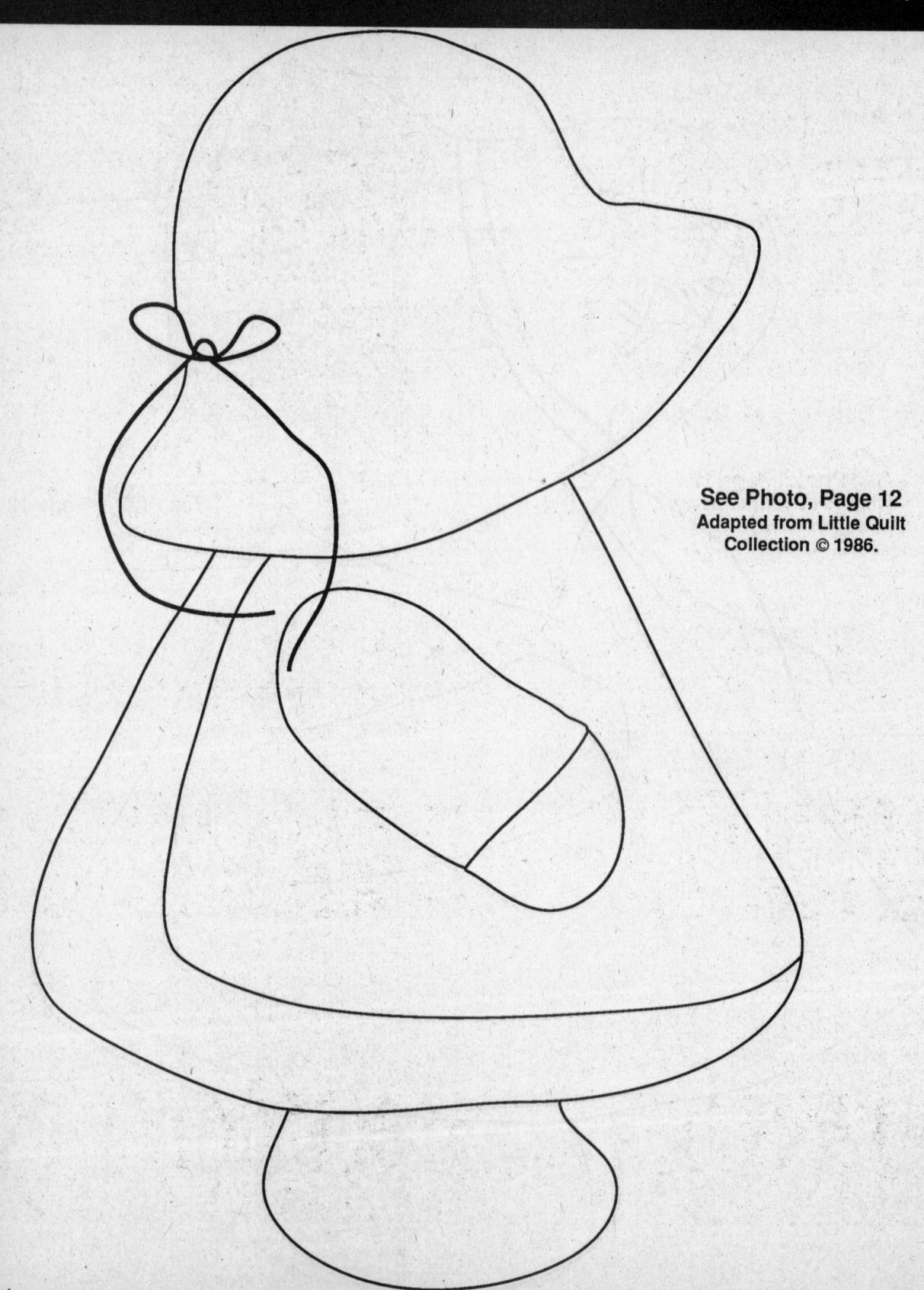

Sunbonnet FAMILY REUNION

A Twin
Lavina E. Miller • Waterford, NJ

See Photo, Page 12
Adapted from Little Quilt
Collection © 1986.

74 Sunbonnet Family Reunion IV

A Twin
Evelyn Kaminsky • Blackwood, NJ

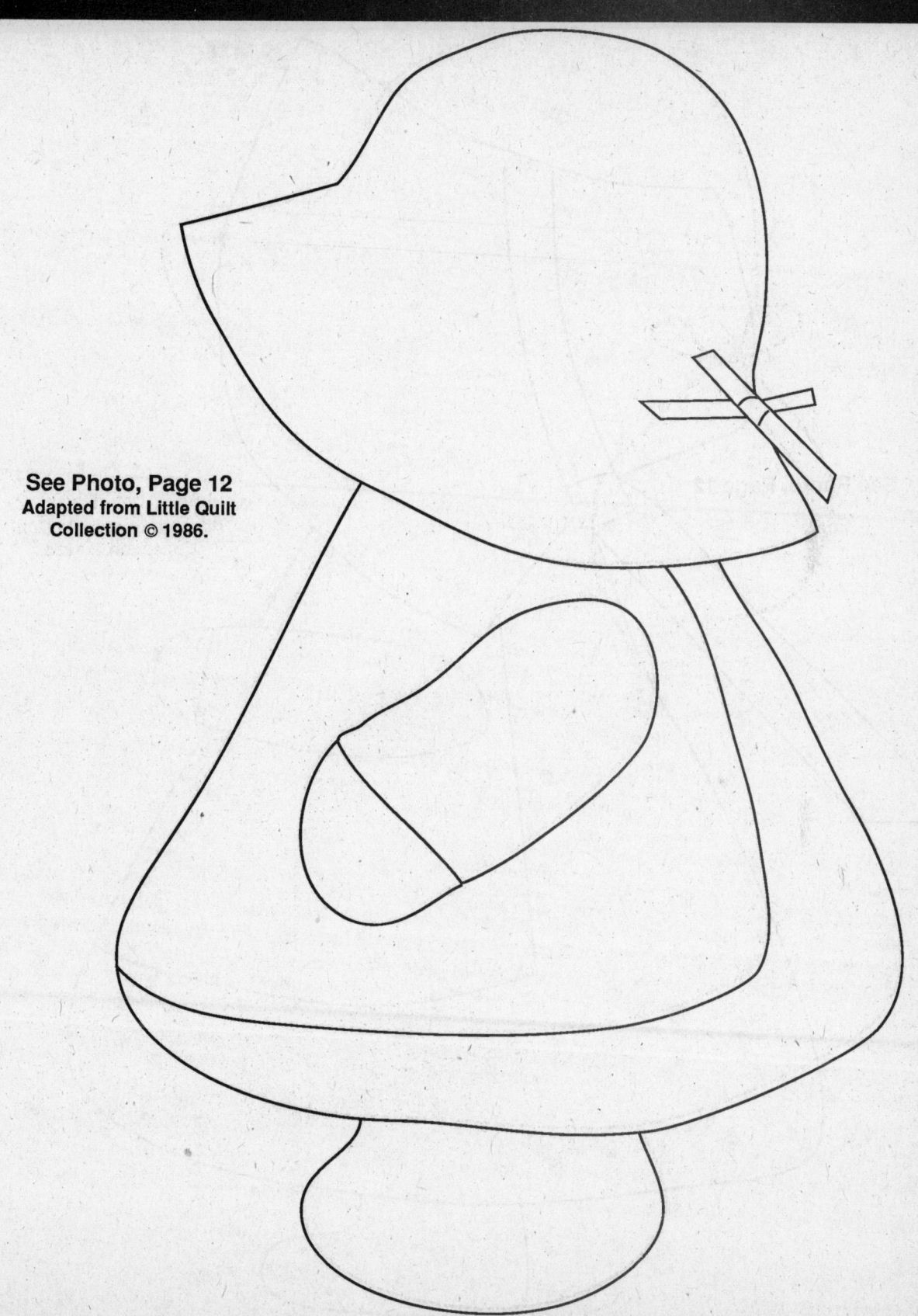

Sunbonnet FAMILY REUNION

See Photo, Page 12
Adapted from Little Quilt Collection © 1986.

Sunbonnet Family Reunion IV

Sunbonnet Blue
Lucille Johnston • Prairie Village, KS

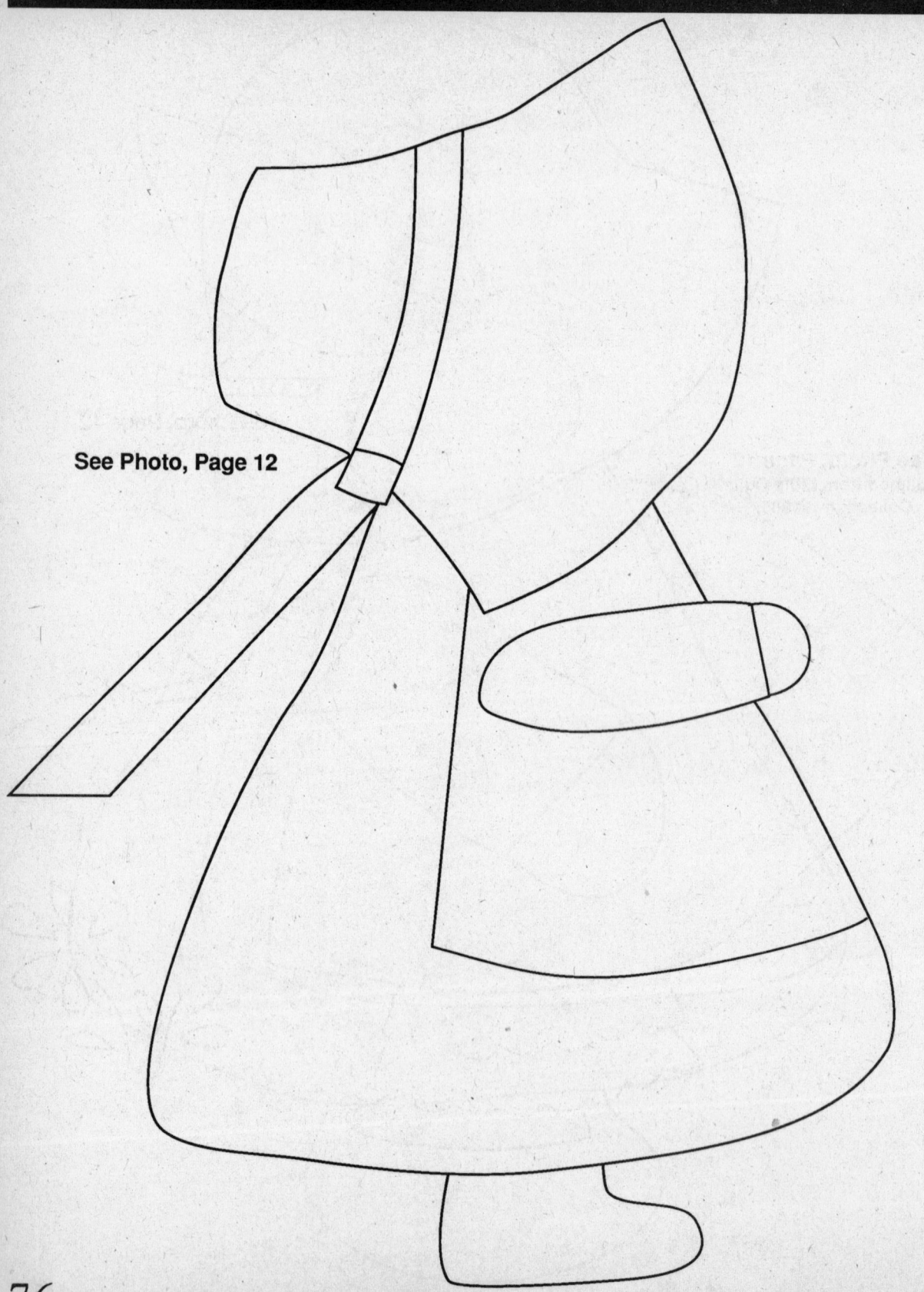

See Photo, Page 12

76 Sunbonnet Family Reunion IV

Lacy Lady
Pat Scott • Kansas City, MO

Sunbonnet FAMILY REUNION

See Photo, Page 12

Sunbonnet Family Reunion IV **77**

Sunbonnet FAMILY REUNION

Grandmother's Little Dutch Girl
Donna A. Duncan • Eminence, KY

See Photo, Page 12

78 Sunbonnet Family Reunion IV

Dressed For Church
Wanda Debolt • S. Daytona, FL

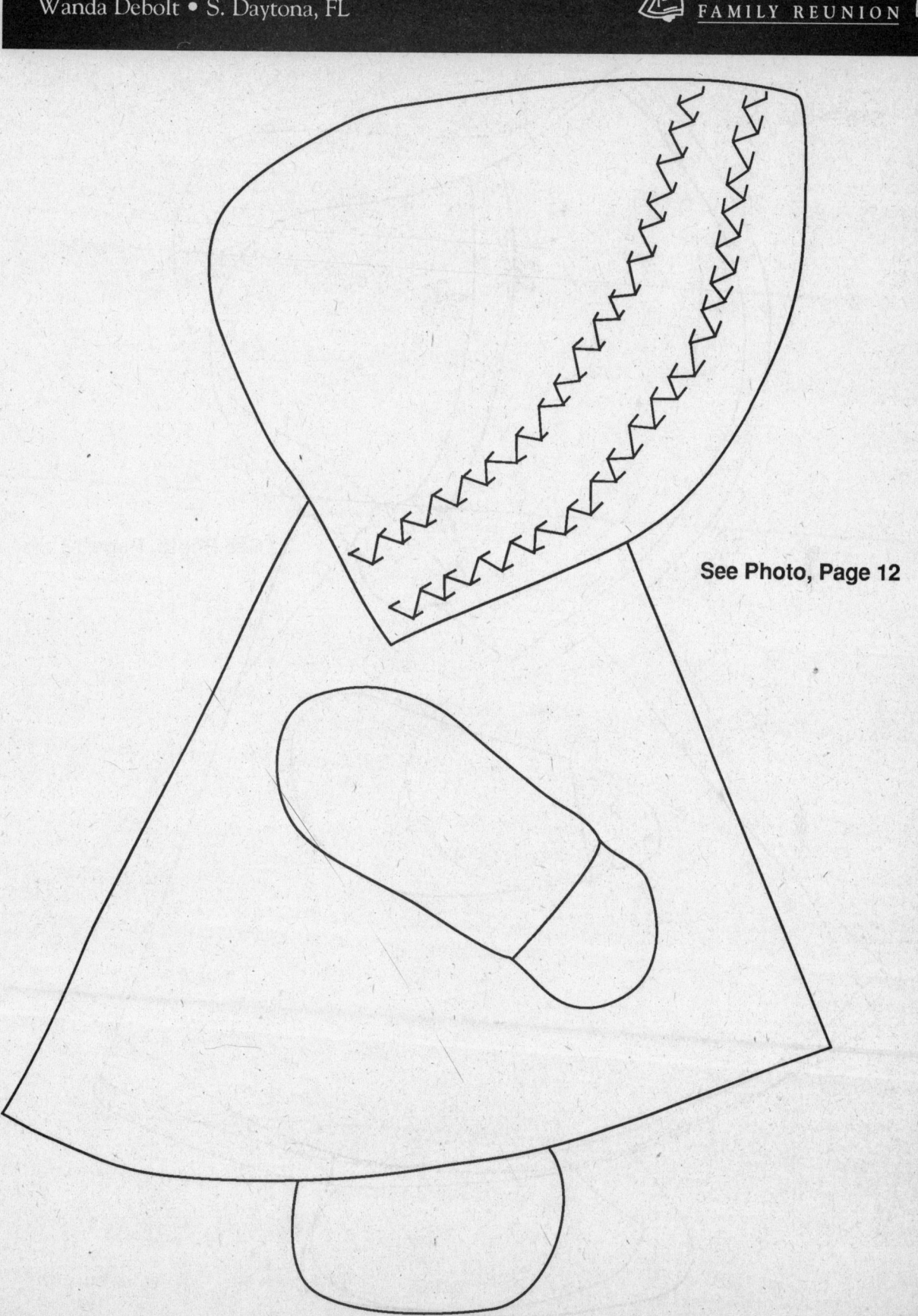

Sunbonnet FAMILY REUNION

See Photo, Page 12

Sunbonnet Family Reunion IV 79

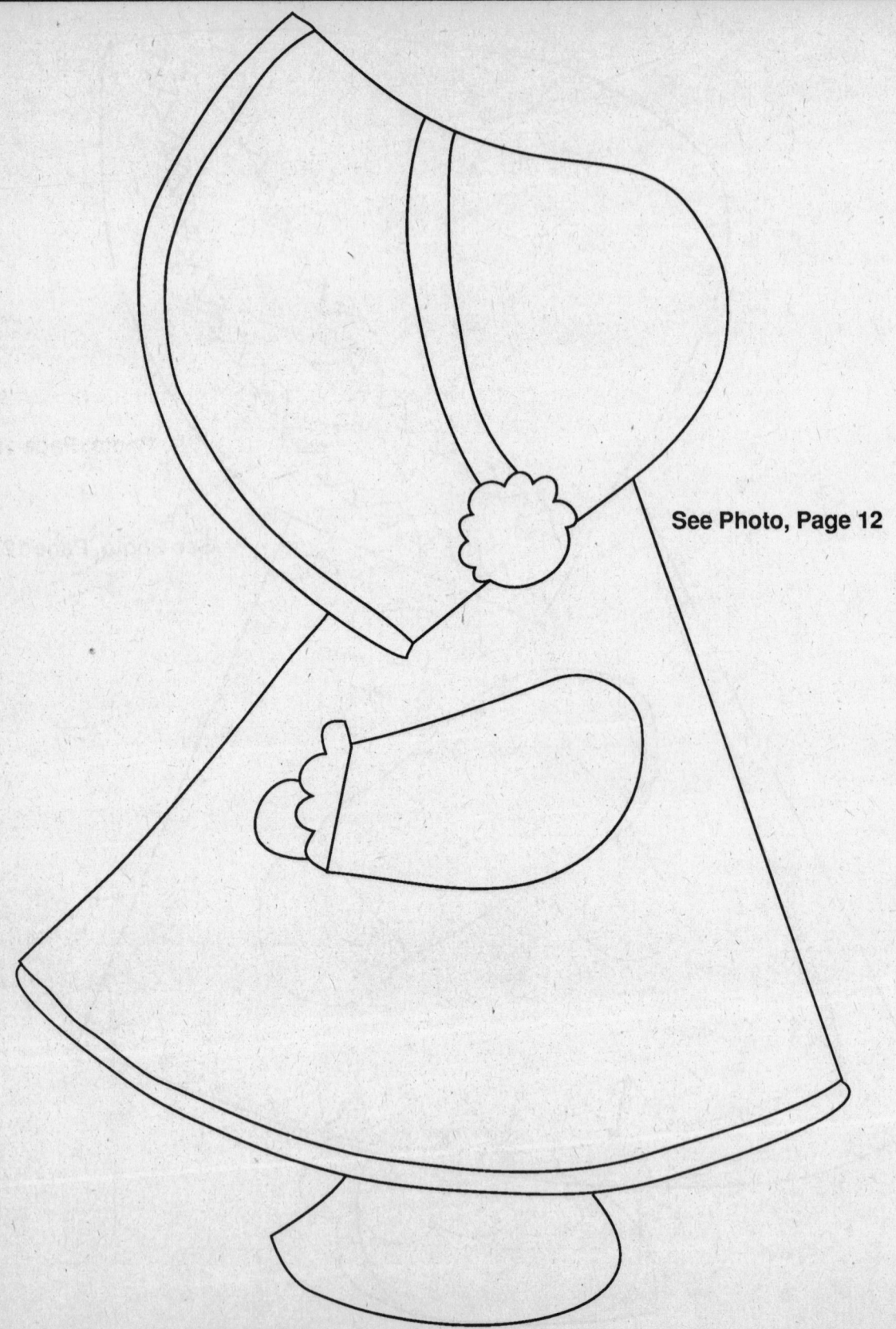

Sunbonnet FAMILY REUNION

Calico Sue
Lois Sours • Drexel, MO

See Photo, Page 12

80 Sunbonnet Family Reunion IV

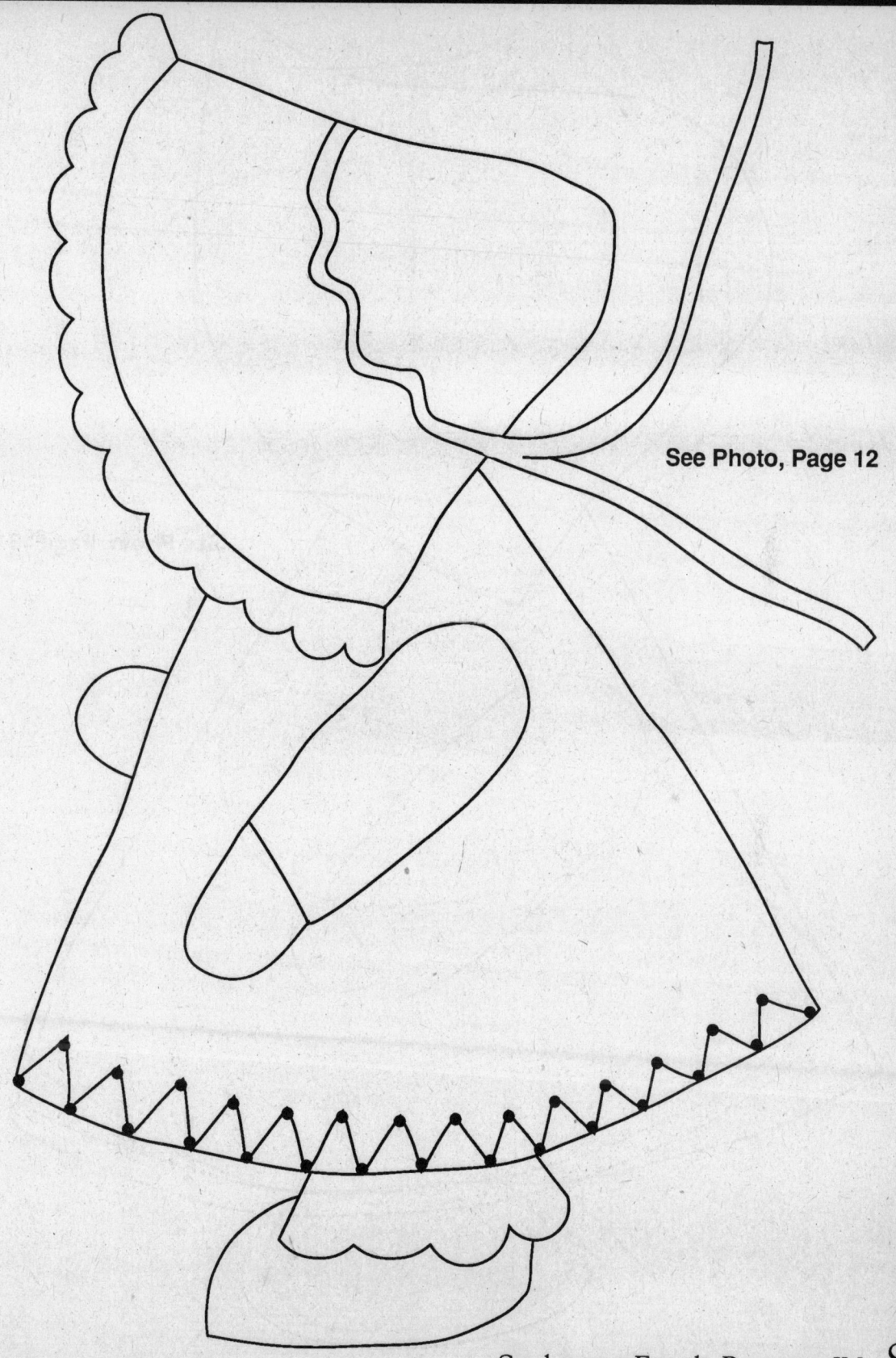

My Sue
Netta Ranney • Overland Park, KS

Sunbonnet FAMILY REUNION

See Photo, Page 12

Sunbonnet Family Reunion IV 81

Sunbonnet Sue
Nova Gaines • Overland Park, KS

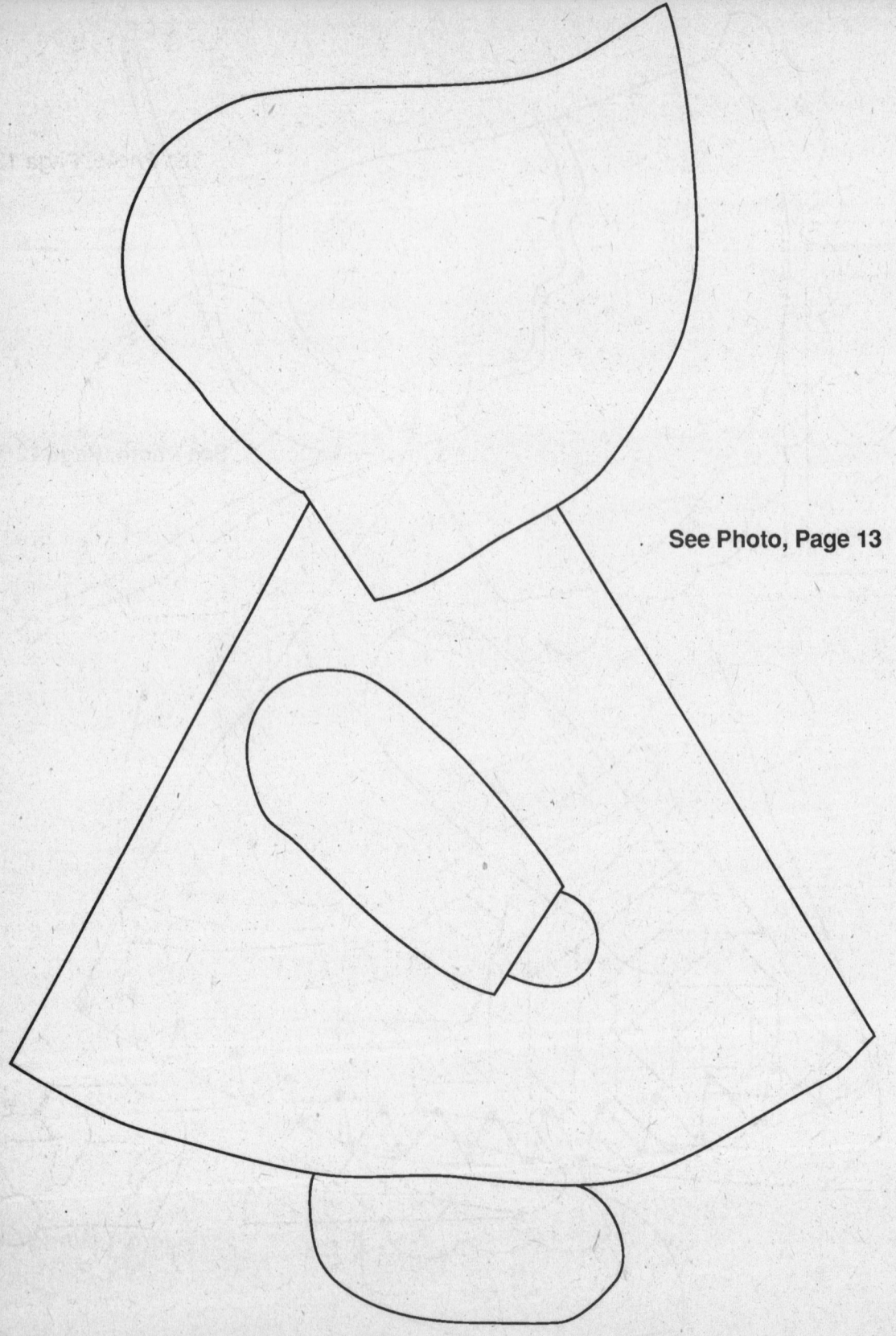

See Photo, Page 13

82 Sunbonnet Family Reunion IV

Favorite Pastime
Lorraine Doyle • Kennewick, WA

Sunbonnet FAMILY REUNION

See Photo, Page 13

Sunbonnet Family Reunion IV 83

Sunbonnet FAMILY REUNION

Too Many Scraps?
Janette Anderson • Irvine, CA

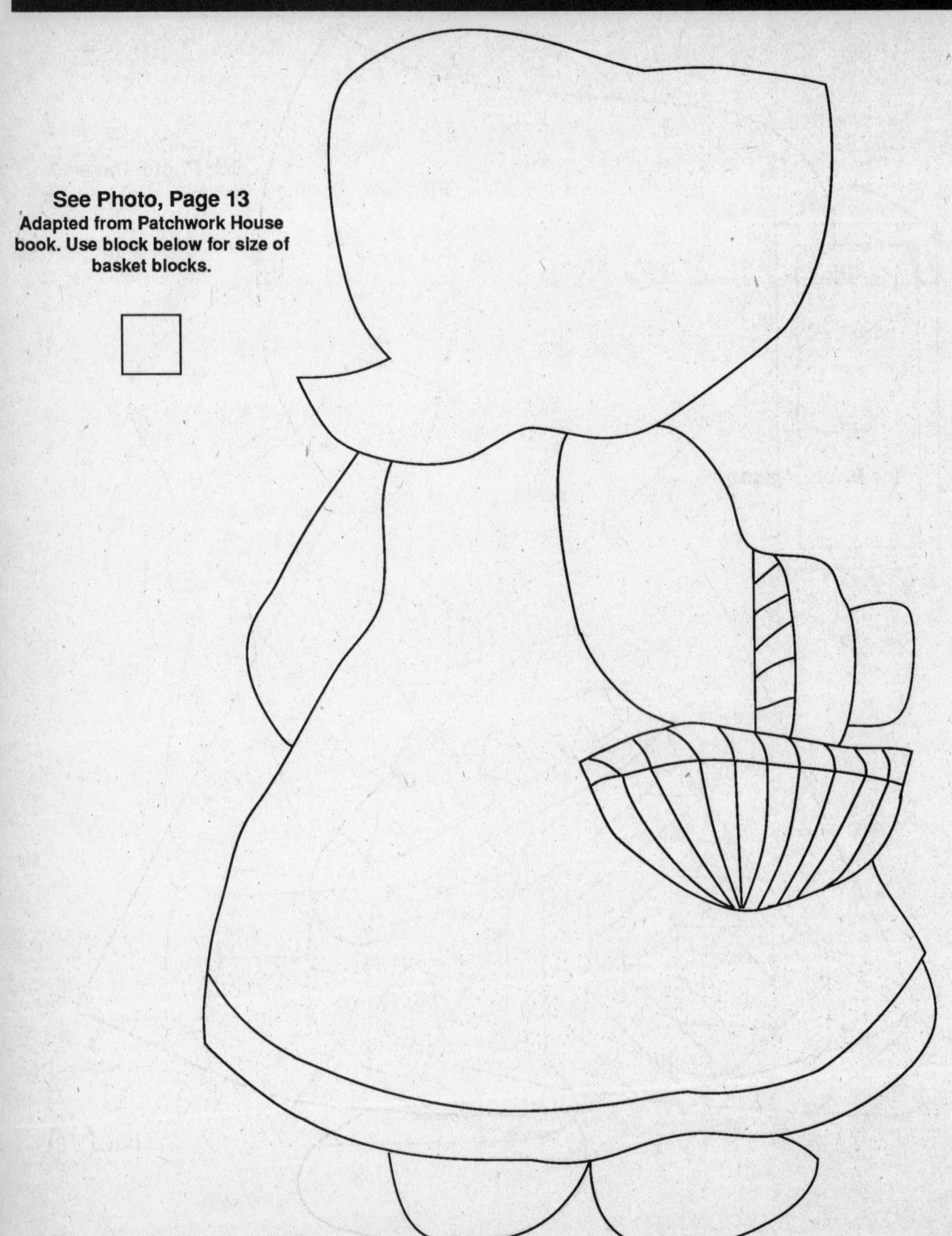

See Photo, Page 13
Adapted from Patchwork House book. Use block below for size of basket blocks.

84 Sunbonnet Family Reunion IV

Little Women
Mary K. Boerger • London, OH

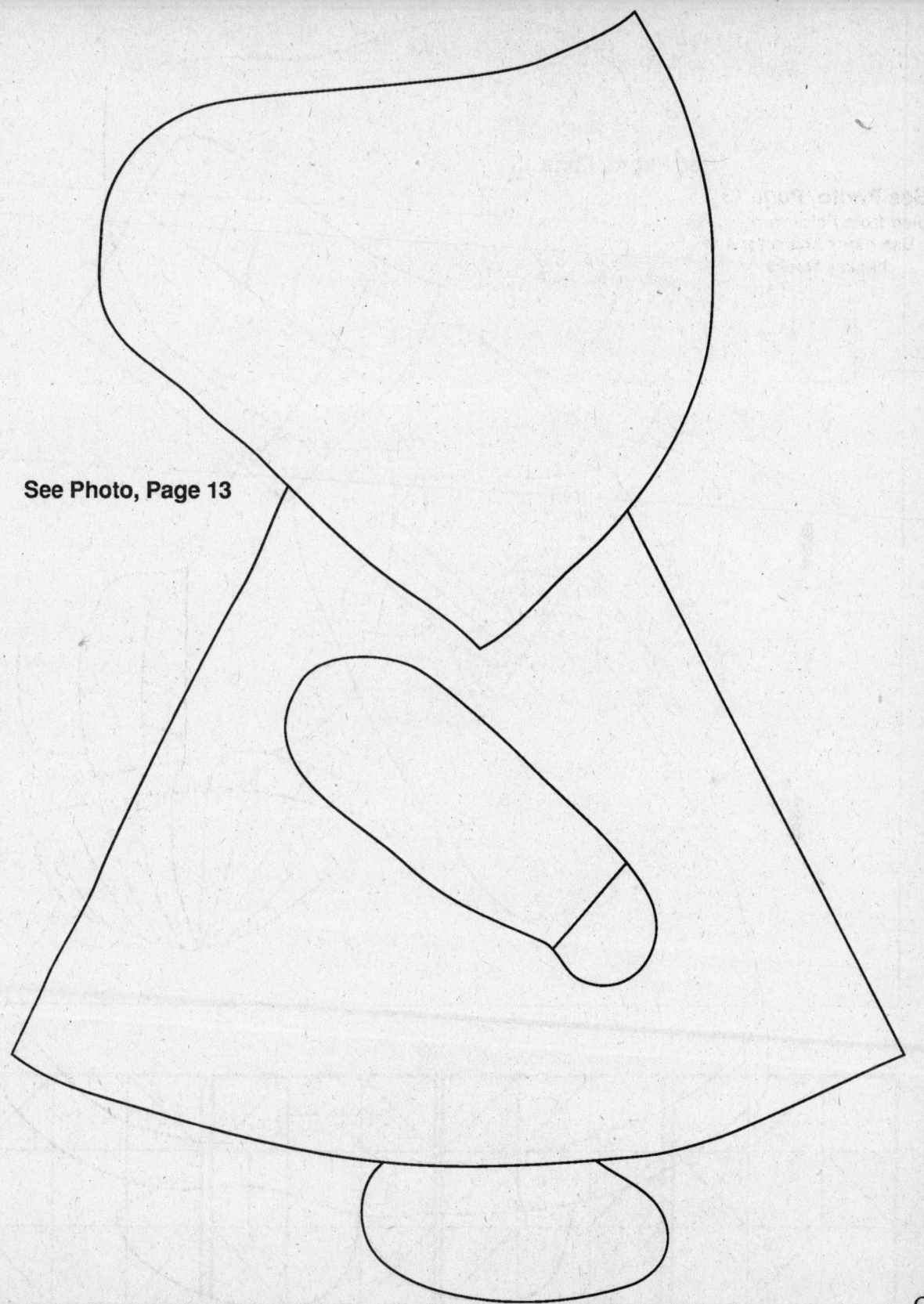

Sunbonnet FAMILY REUNION

See Photo, Page 13

Sunbonnet Family Reunion IV 85

Sunbonnet FAMILY REUNION

Quilt Dreamer
Rose Marie Baab • Wooster, OH

See Photo, Page 13

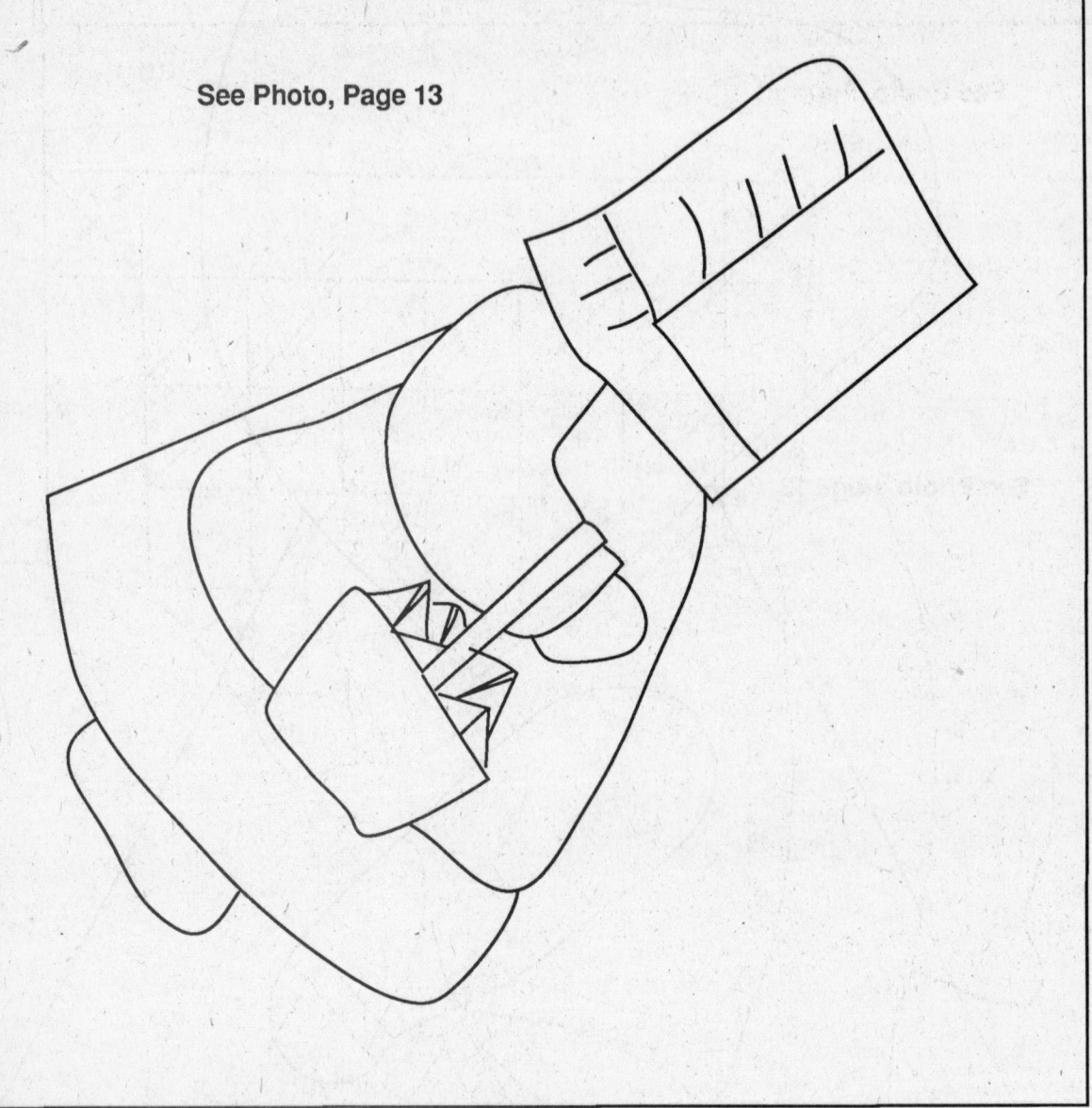

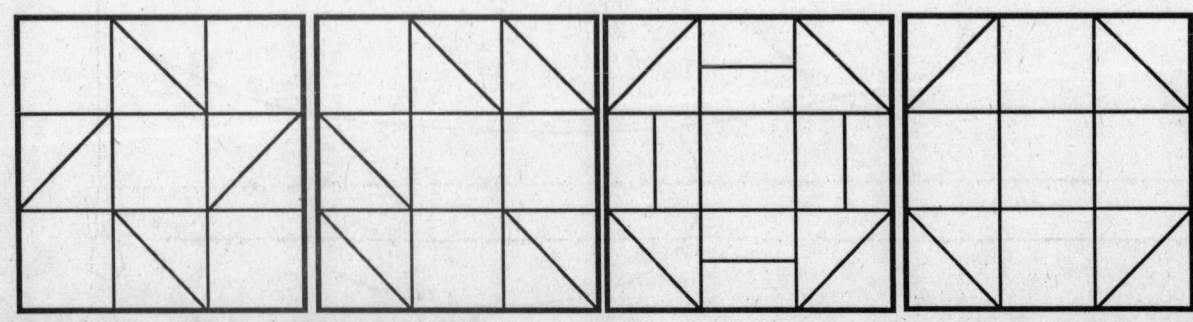

86 Sunbonnet Family Reunion IV

Amish Monday
Mary R. Jones • Bulverde, TX

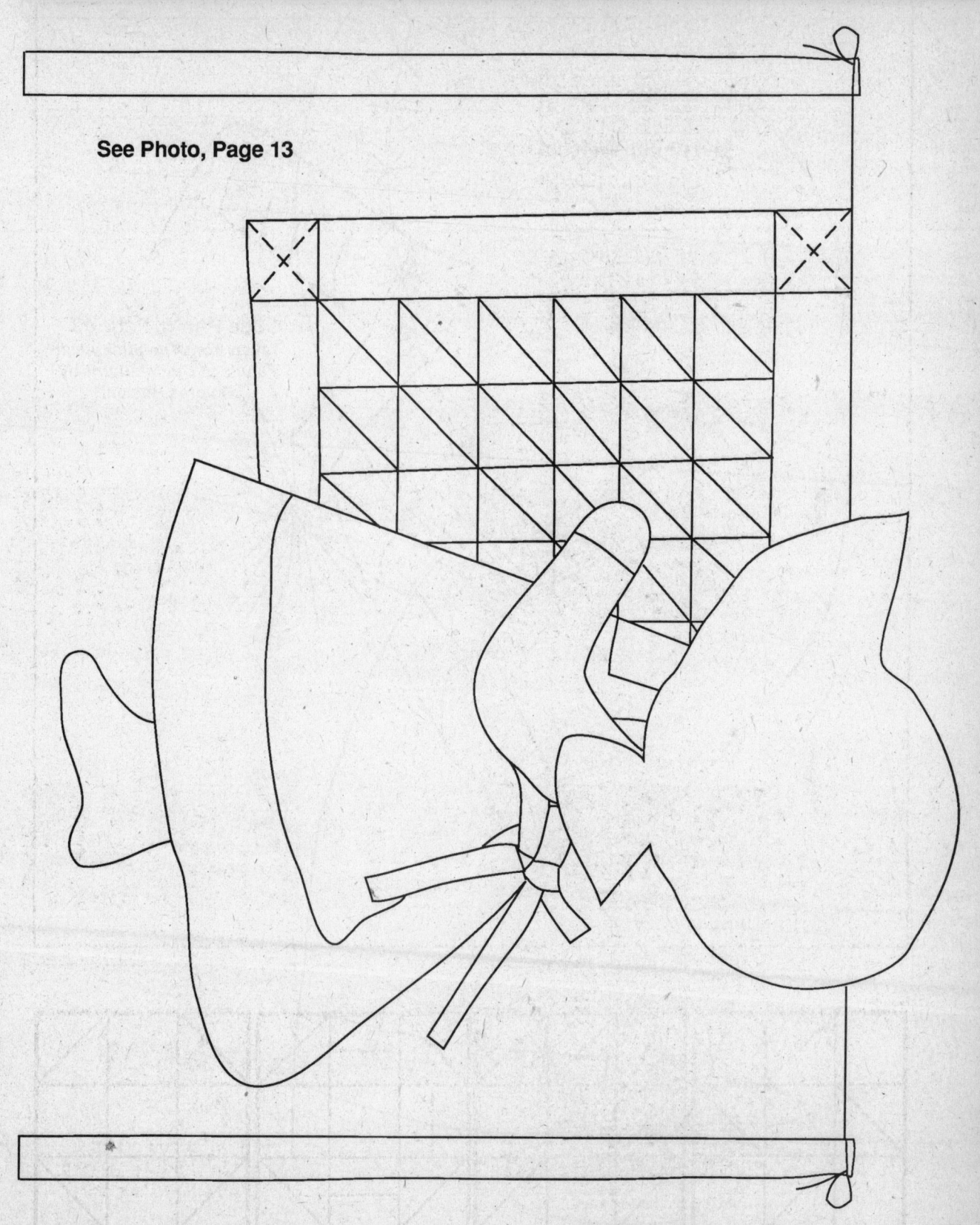

See Photo, Page 13

Sunbonnet Family Reunion IV 87

Sunbonnet FAMILY REUNION

Smell The Flowers
Beatrice J. Woodland • Yreka, CA

See Photo, Page 13
Taken from *The Sunbonnet Family of Quilt Patterns* by Dolores Hinson.

88 Sunbonnet Family Reunion IV

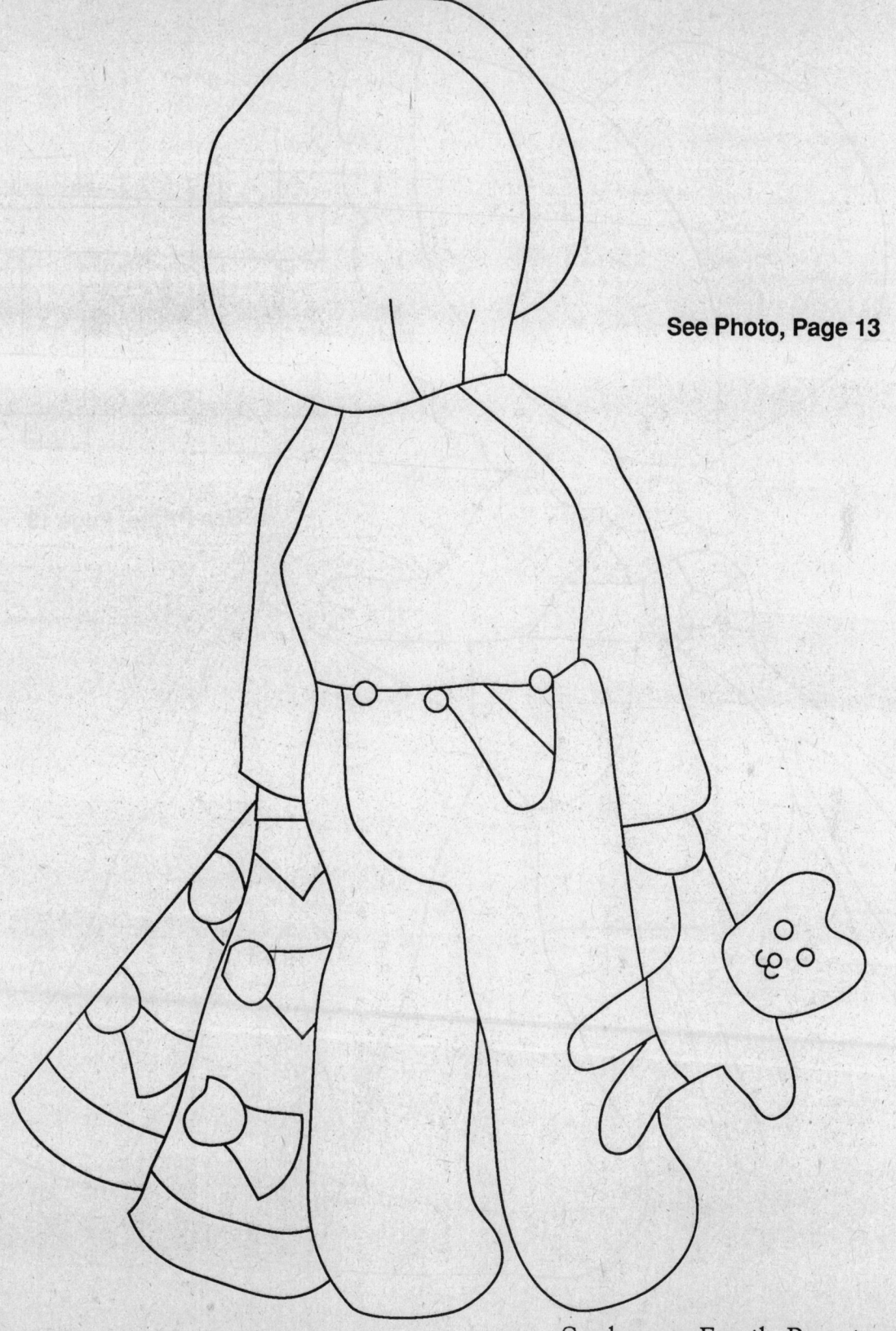

Sunbonnet Sue Goes To Bed
Linda M. Throckmorton • Cutler, ME

See Photo, Page 13

Sunbonnet Family Reunion IV

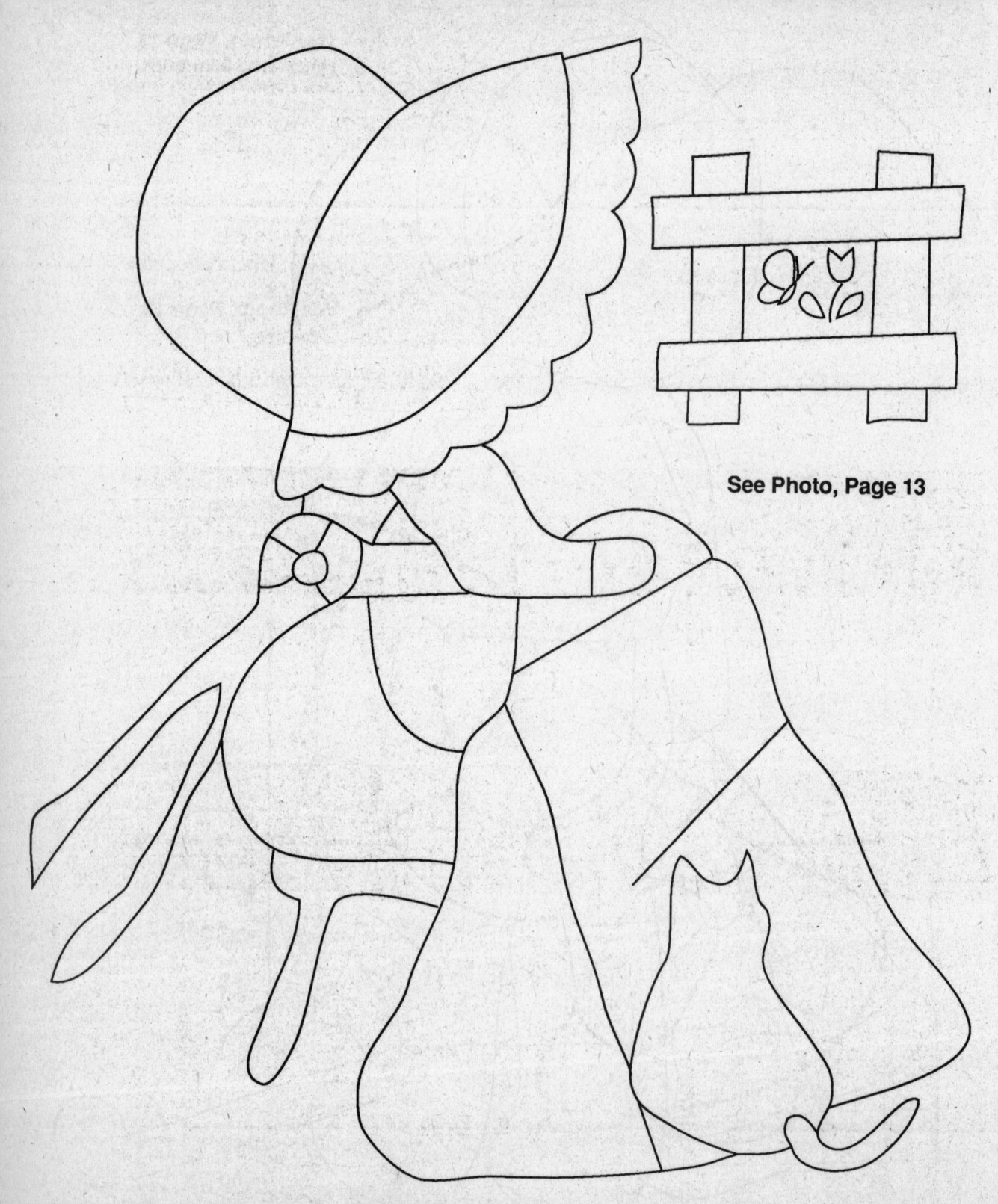

Sunbonnet FAMILY REUNION

Quilt Lady
Helen Beer • Solon, OH

See Photo, Page 13

90 Sunbonnet Family Reunion IV

Upsy Daisy
Kay Lanham • Lander, WY

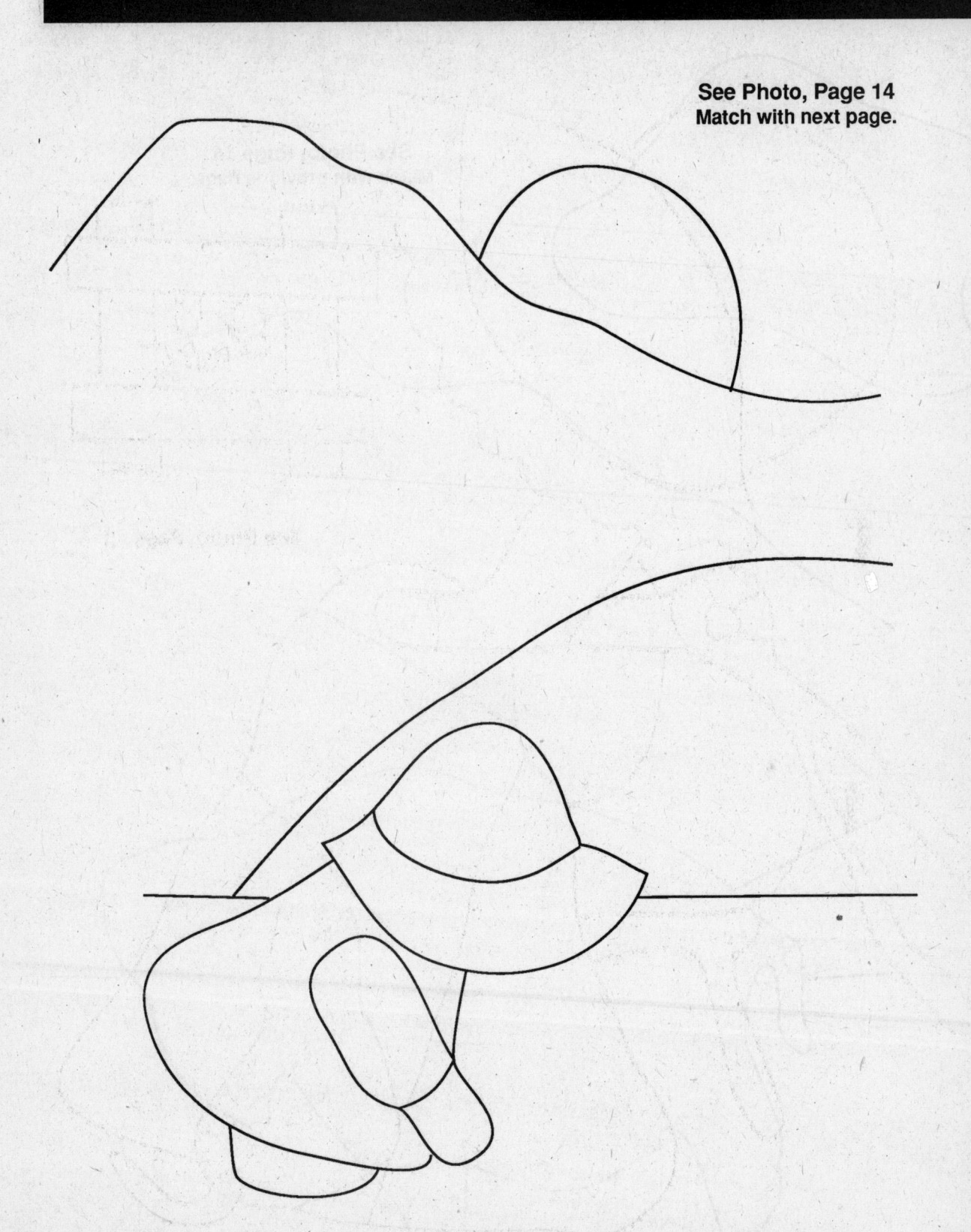

See Photo, Page 14
Match with next page.

Sunbonnet Family Reunion IV 91

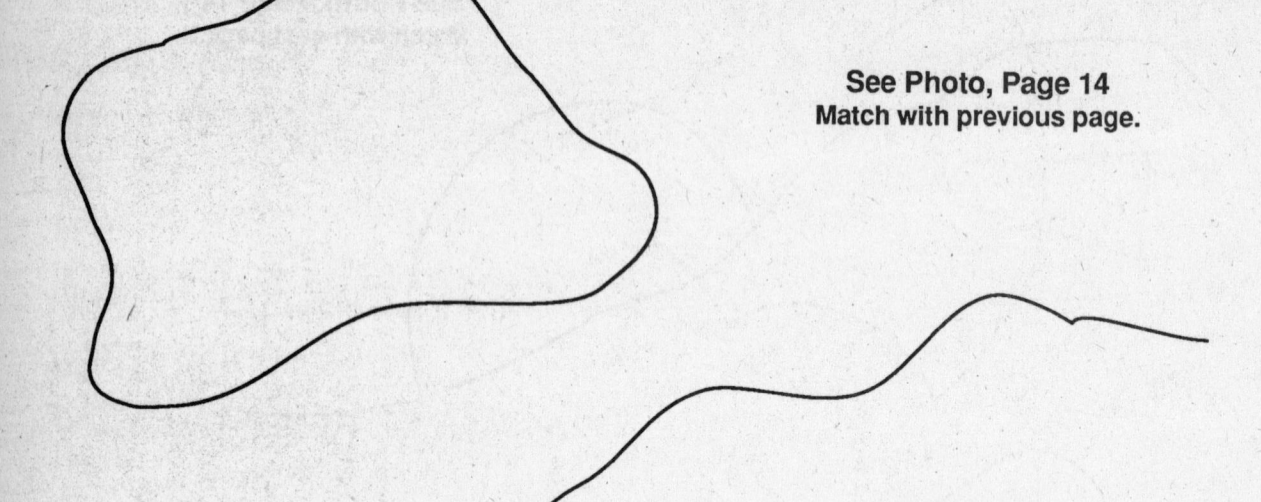

Sunbonnet FAMILY REUNION

**See Photo, Page 14
Match with previous page.**

92 Sunbonnet Family Reunion IV

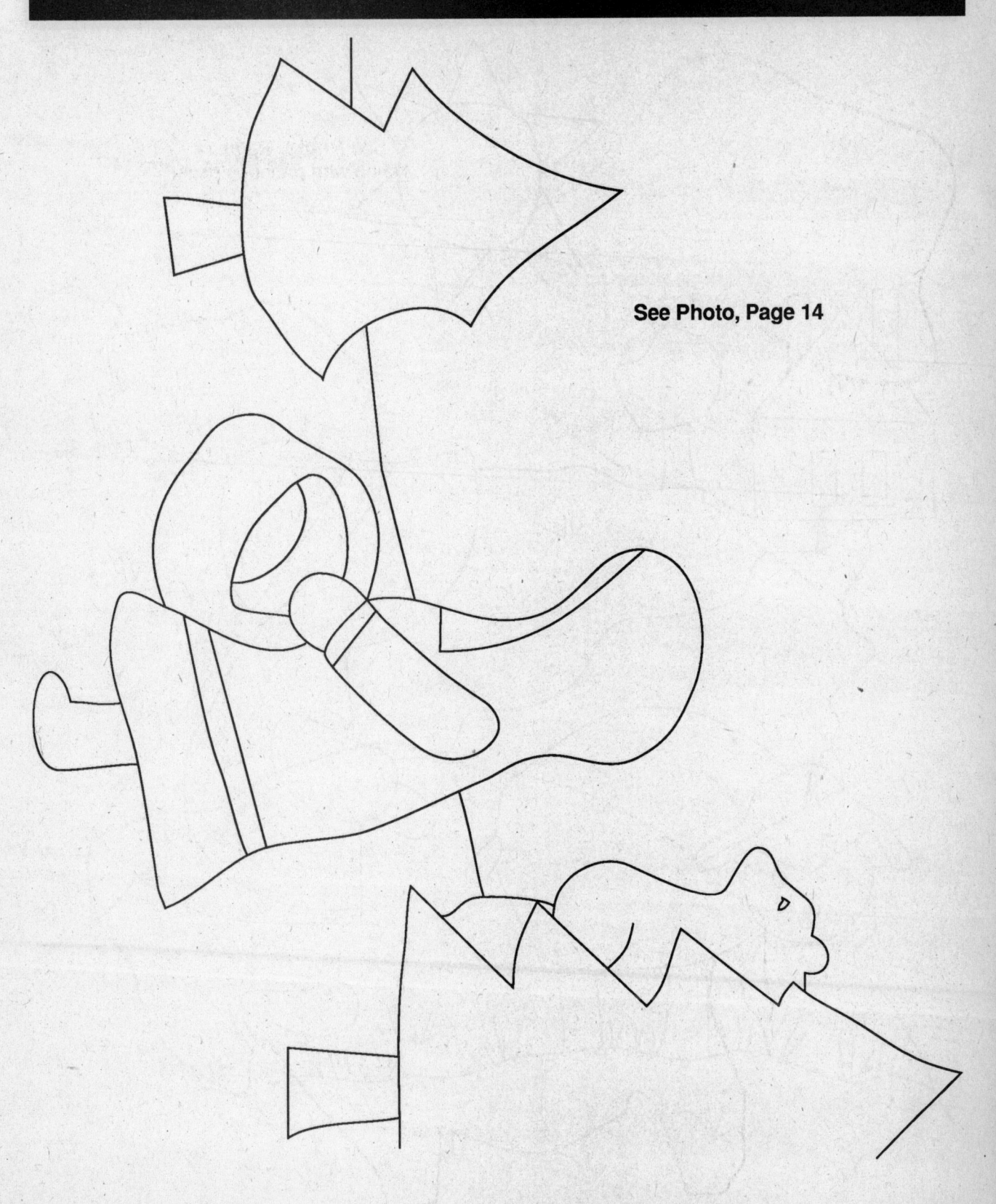

Sunbonnet Sue Visits Alaska
Carol Rhoades • Anchorage, AK

See Photo, Page 14

Sunbonnet Family Reunion

Sunbonnet Sue Has A Lamb Too!
Martie Culp • Wheeling, WV

See Photo, Page 14

94 Sunbonnet Family Reunion IV

Playtime
Phyllis Saelens • Seattle, WA

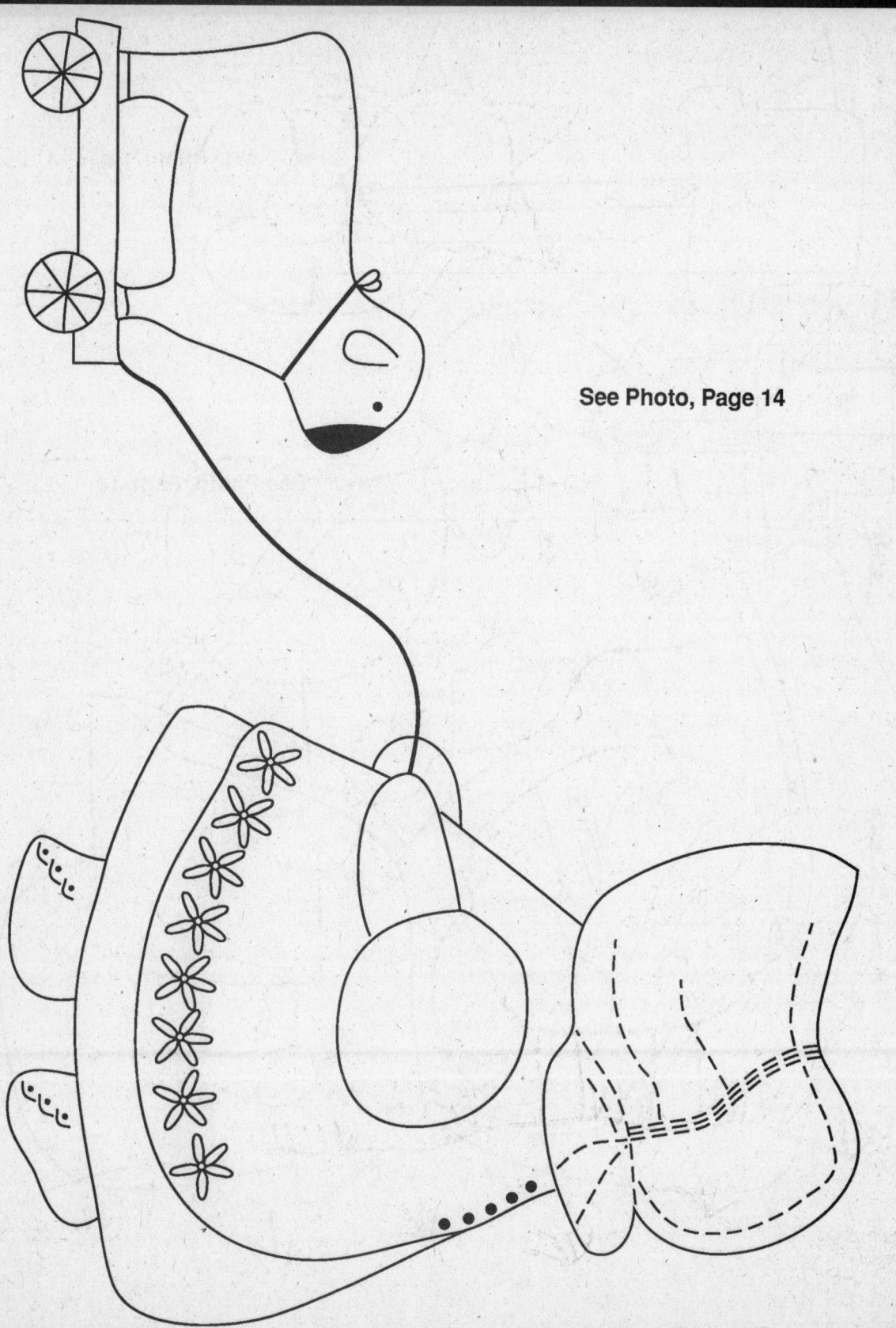

Sunbonnet FAMILY REUNION

See Photo, Page 14

Sunbonnet Family Reunion IV 95

Sunbonnet Girl With Bunny
Muriel Spencer • Rio Dell, CA

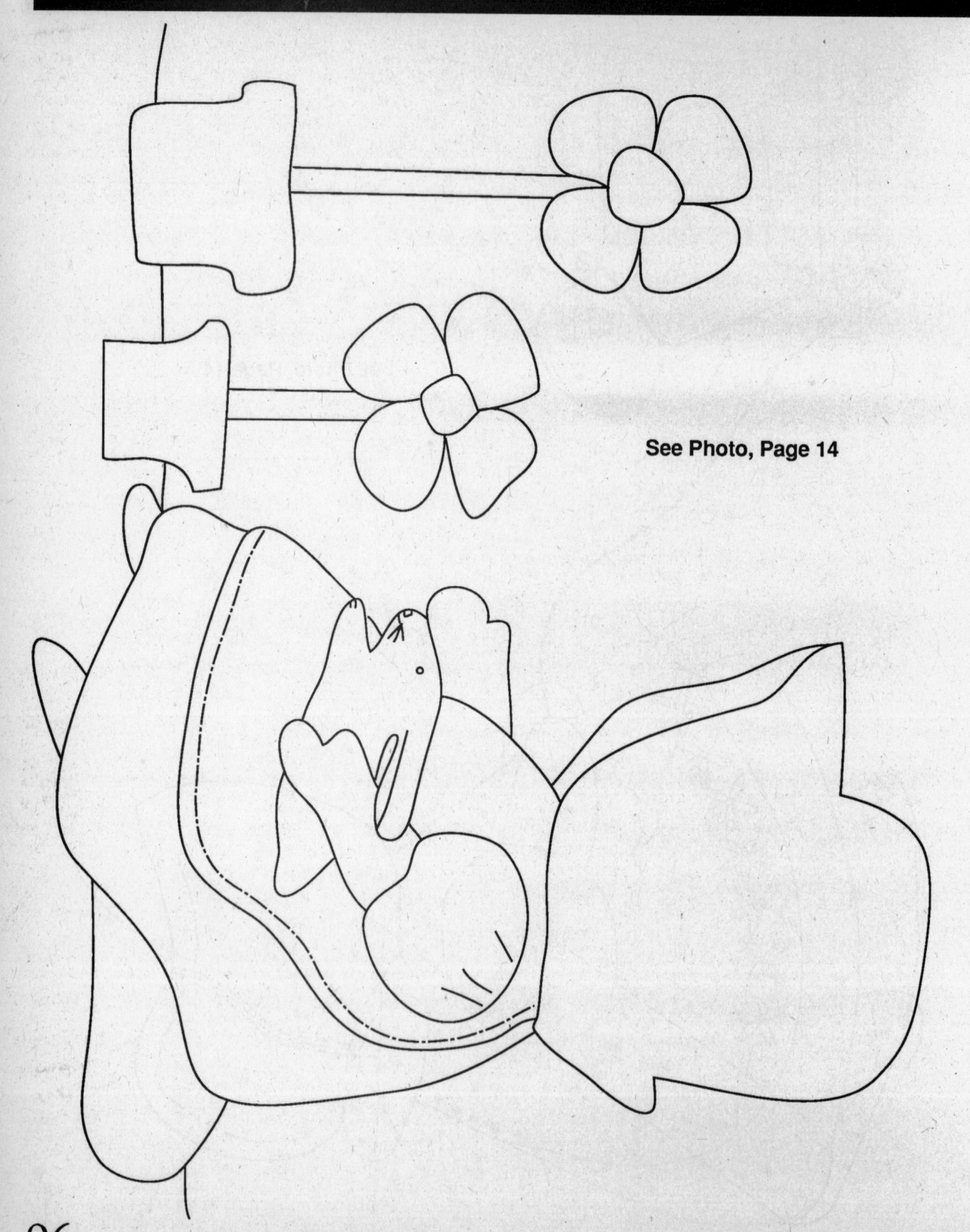

See Photo, Page 14

96 Sunbonnet Family Reunion IV

Feeding The Kids
Linda McCuean • New Galilee, PA

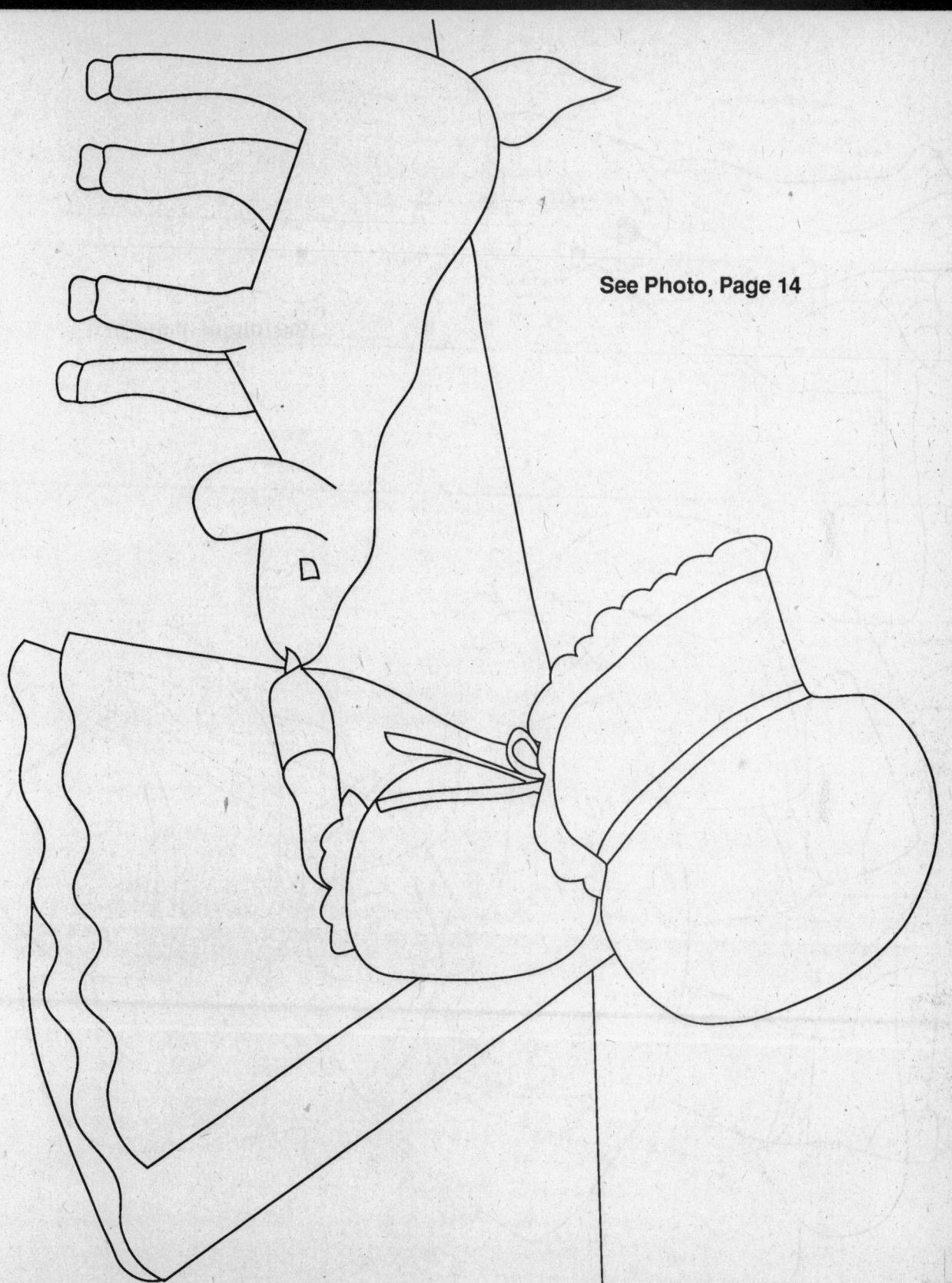

See Photo, Page 14

Sunbonnet Family Reunion IV

Sunbonnet FAMILY REUNION

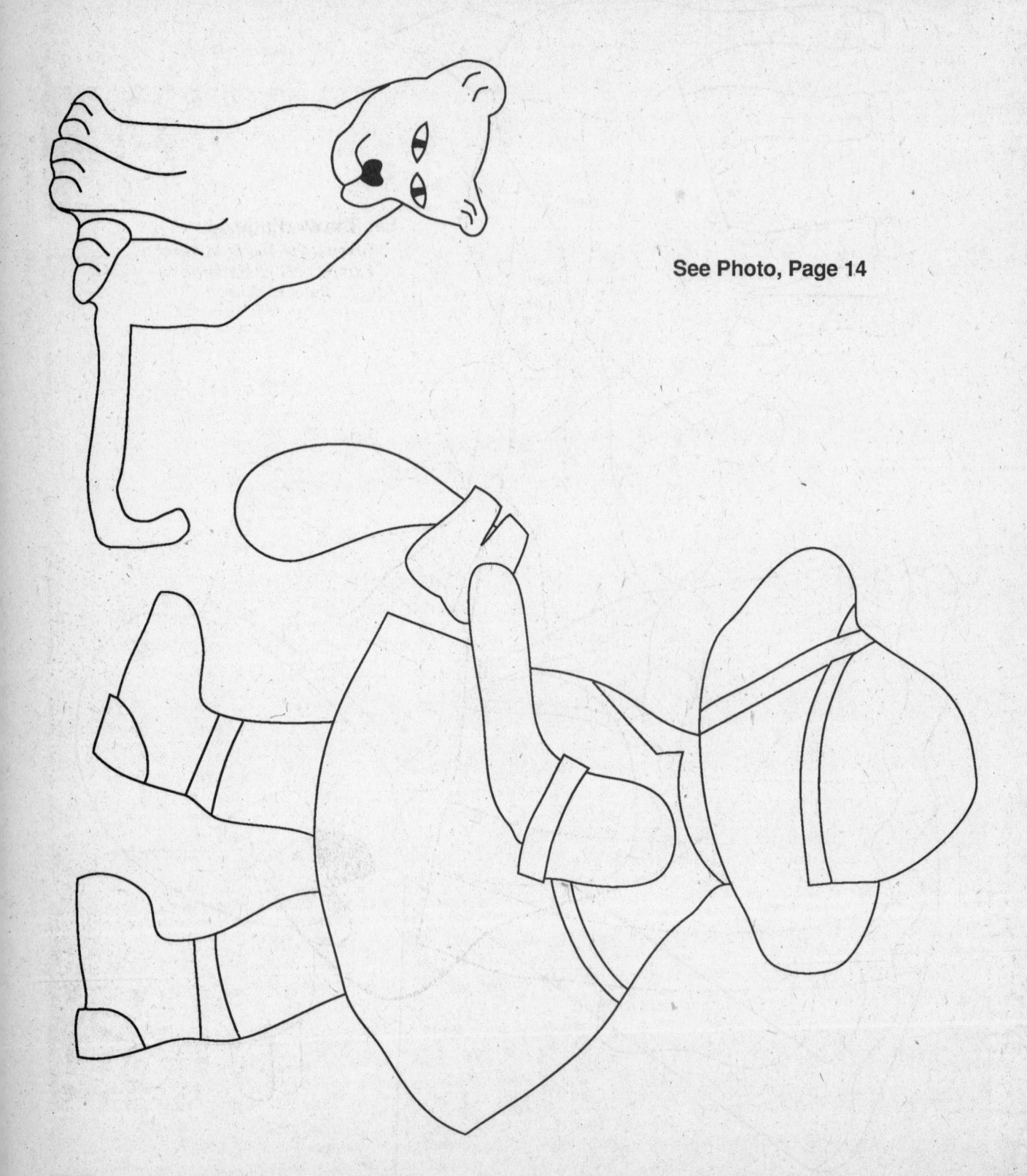

Safari Sue
Leona E. Price • Florissant, MO

See Photo, Page 14

98 Sunbonnet Family Reunion IV

Lovin' Lucy
Hazel Frazier • Calumet, OK

Sunbonnet FAMILY REUNION

See Photo, Page 14
Taken from *The Sunbonnet Family of Quilt Patterns* **by Dolores Hinson.**

Sunbonnet Family Reunion IV

Sunbonnet FAMILY REUNION

Sunbonnet Fields
Sybil Scales • Lawrence, KS

See Photo, Page 14
Match with next page.

100 Sunbonnet Family Reunion IV

Sunbonnet FAMILY REUNION

See Photo, Page 14
Match with previous page.

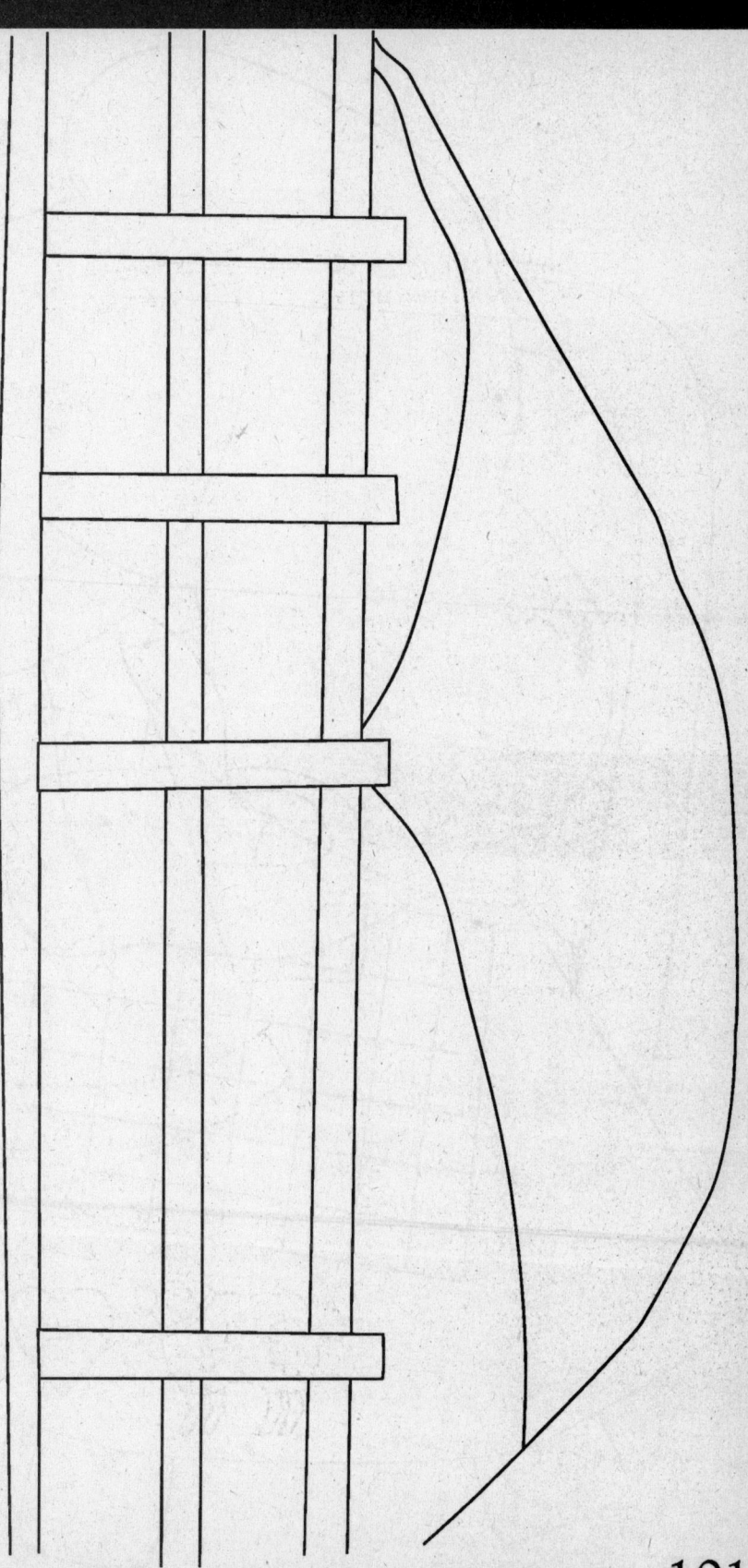

Sunbonnet Family Reunion IV 101

Sunbonnet FAMILY REUNION

Amish Sunbonnet Sue Quilting
Susan N. Knutsen • Emmetsburg, IA

See Photo, Page 15

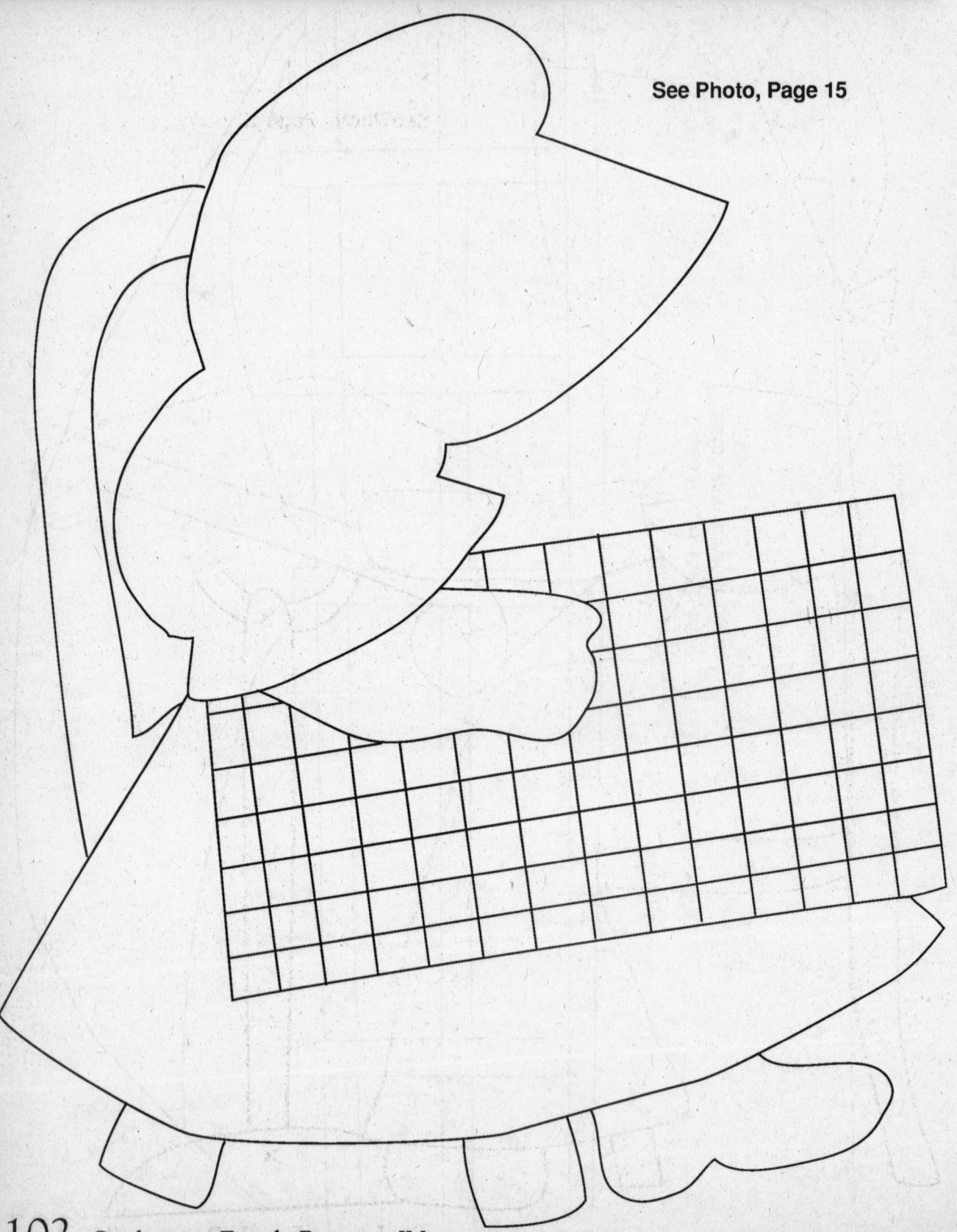

102 Sunbonnet Family Reunion IV

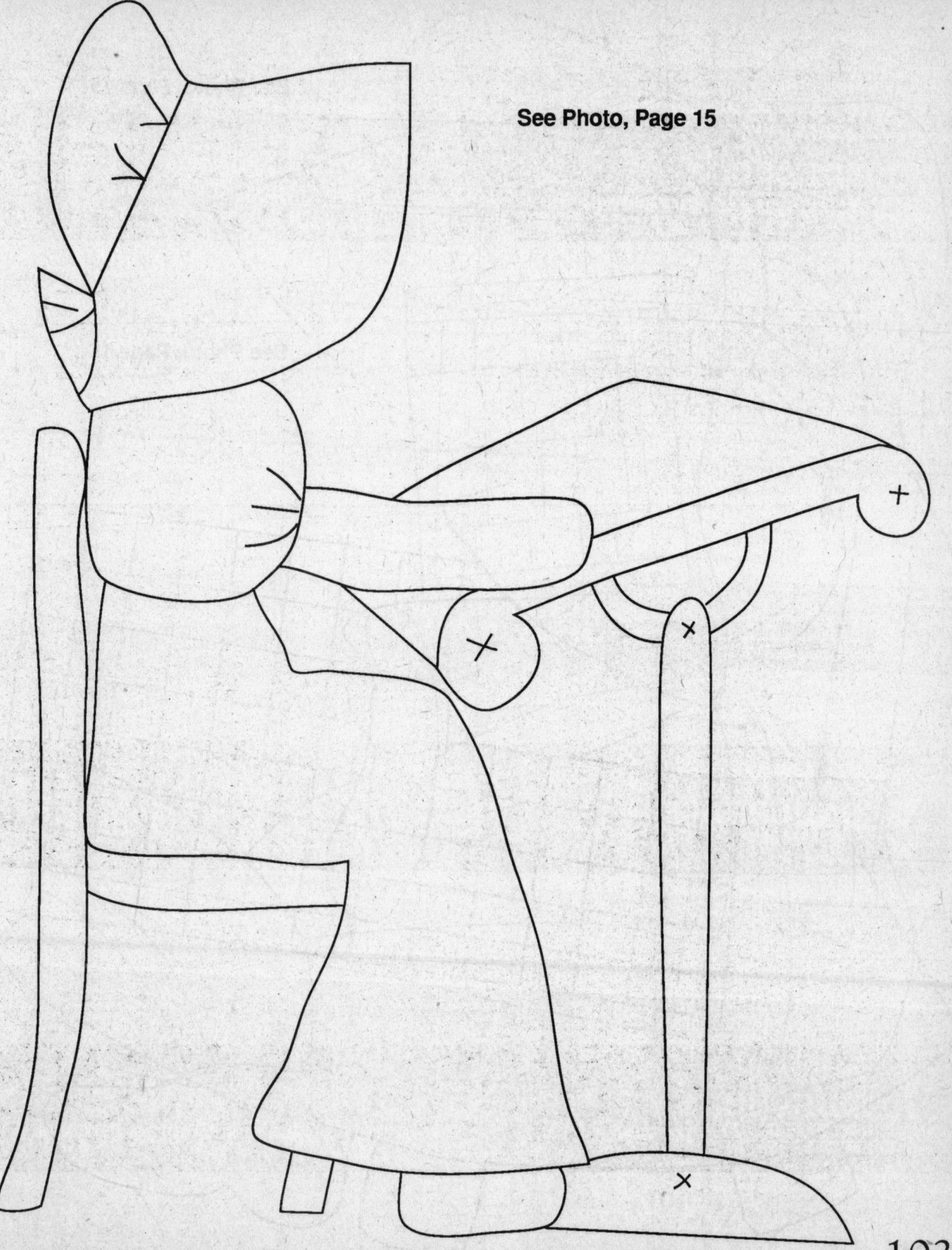

Happy Hours At Home
Claudine Langford • Dimmitt, TX

See Photo, Page 15

Quilting Lady
Lillian Michalez • Vienna, OH

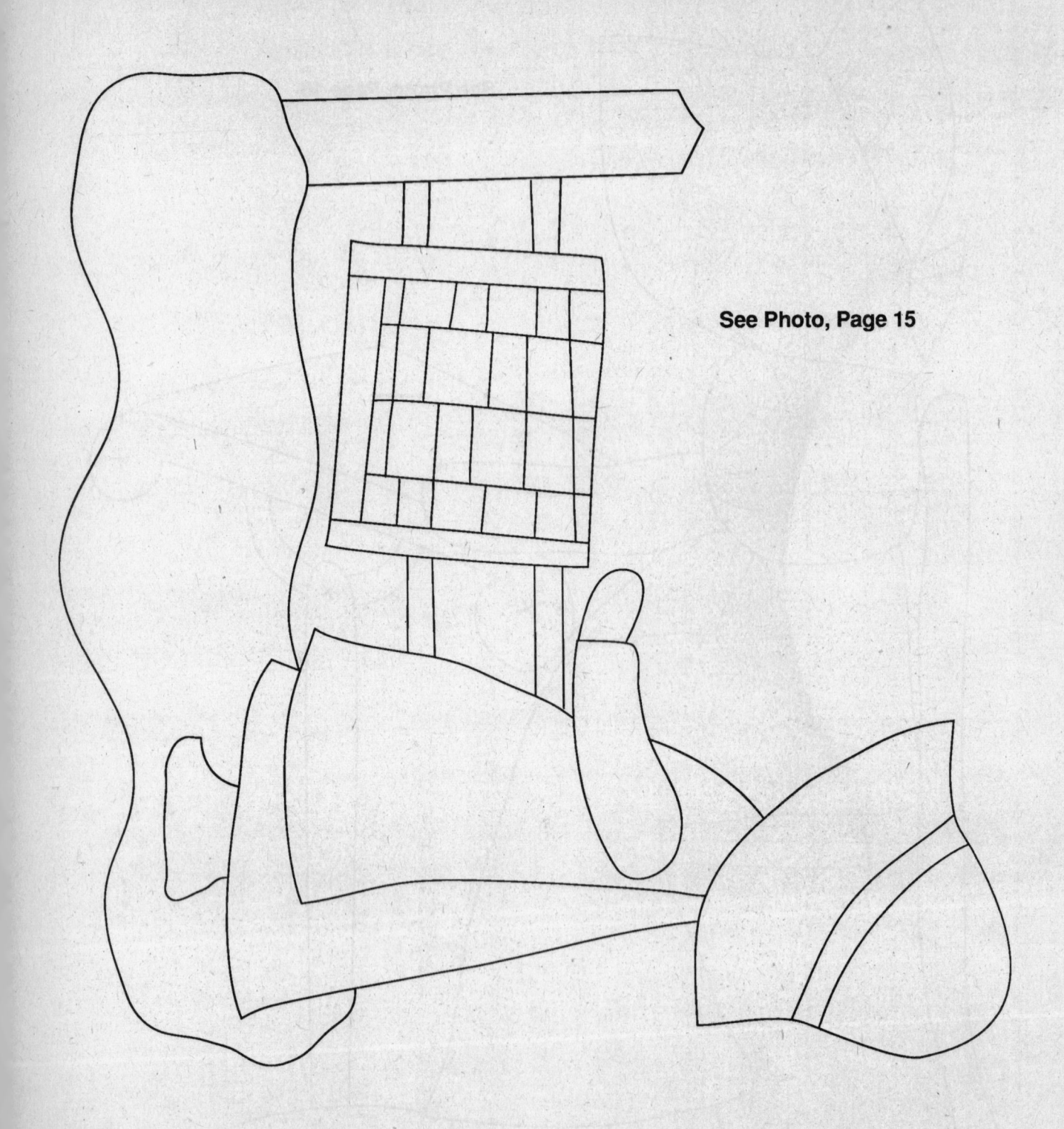

See Photo, Page 15

104 Sunbonnet Family Reunion IV

Just A Few More Basting Stitches
Molly Wilson • Gonzales, TX

Sunbonnet FAMILY REUNION

See Photo, Page 15

Sunbonnet Family Reunion IV 105

Sunbonnet Sue, Quilt Show Judge
Patricia Andersen • Lincoln, NE

See Photo, Page 15
Match with next page.
Taken from *Stitch 'N Sew Quilts*
April 1988.

Sunbonnet Family Reunion

See Photo, Page 15
Match with previous page.
Taken from *Stitch 'N Sew Quilts*
April 1988.

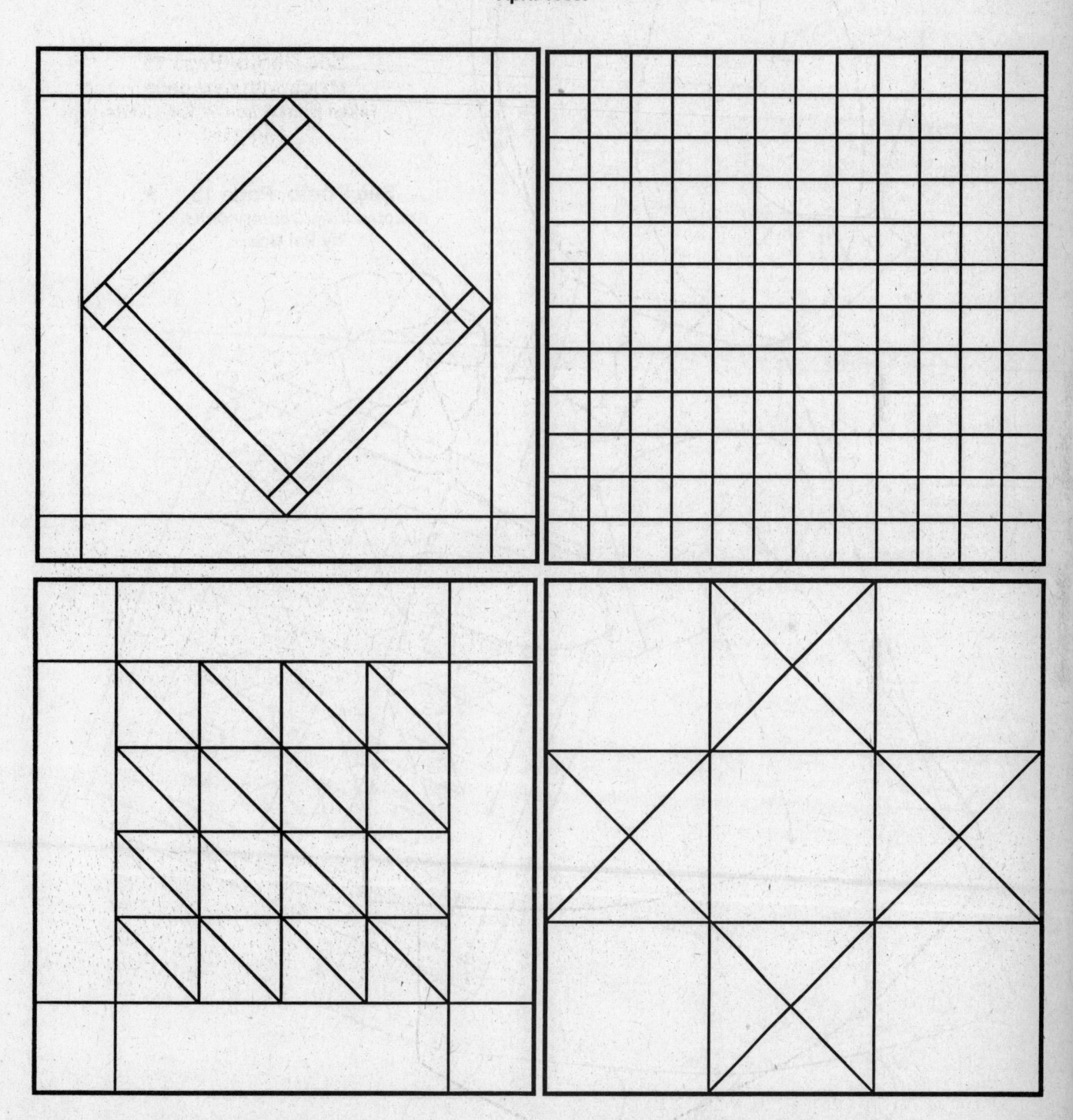

Sunbonnet Family Reunion IV 107

Sunbonnet FAMILY REUNION

Sue's Star
Hazel L. Abel • Kennewick, WA

See Photo, Page 15
Adapted from *Country Children* by Pat Cox.

108 Sunbonnet Family Reunion IV

Toyroom Trotters
Ardeth Sveadas • Sparta, MI

Sunbonnet
FAMILY REUNION

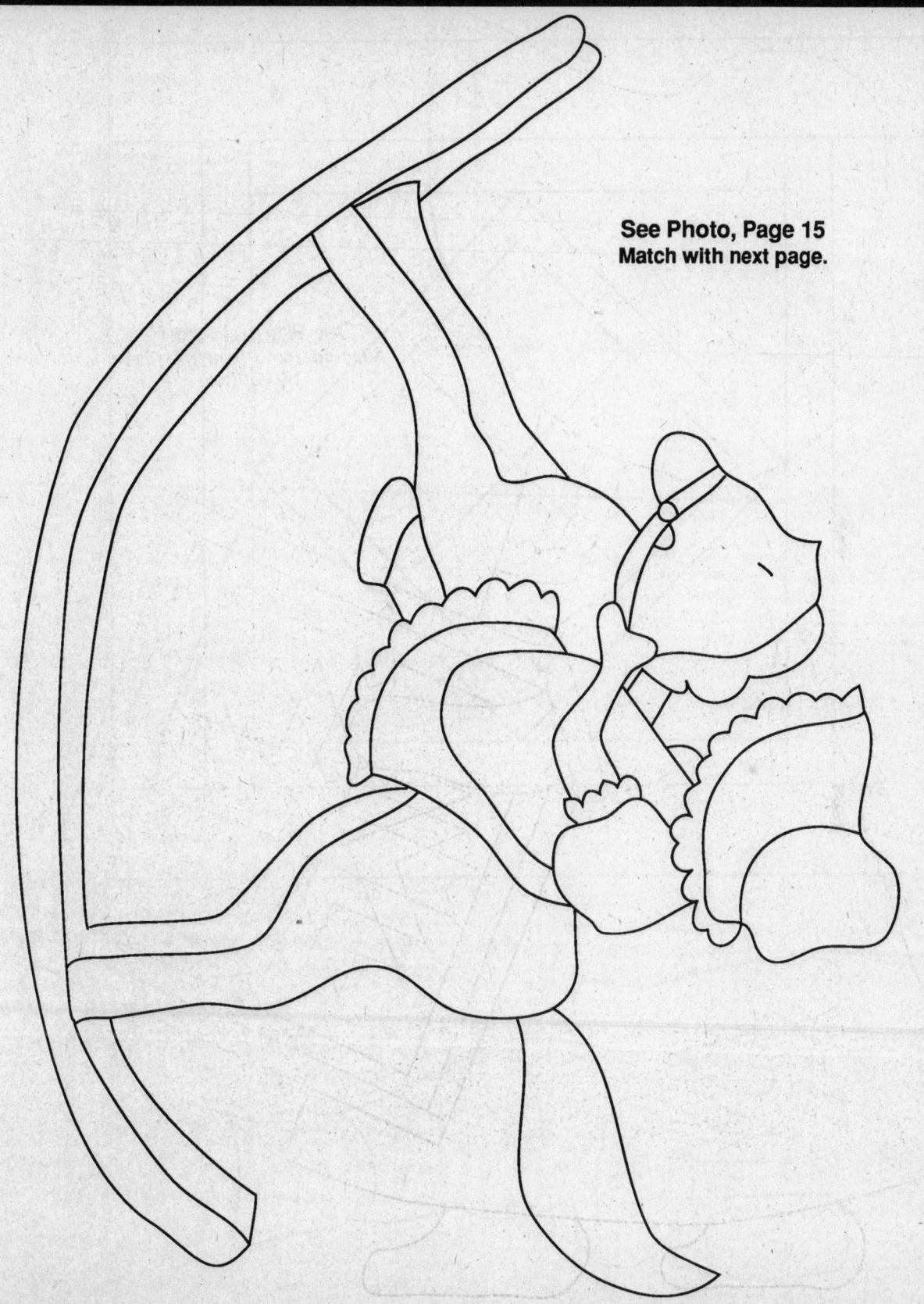

See Photo, Page 15
Match with next page.

Sunbonnet Family Reunion IV

Sunbonnet FAMILY REUNION

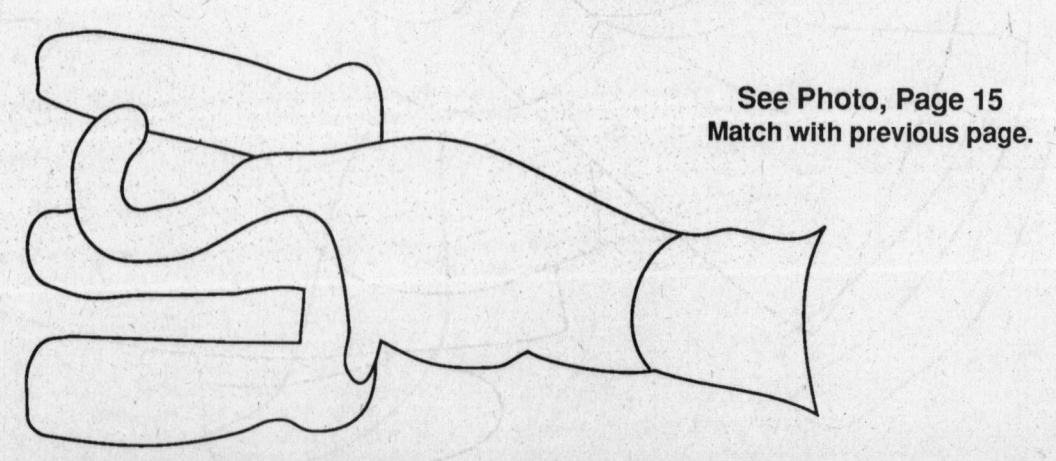

See Photo, Page 15
Match with previous page.

110 Sunbonnet Family Reunion IV

Sue Goes To Quilt Guild Meeting
Opal Frey • Arvada, CO

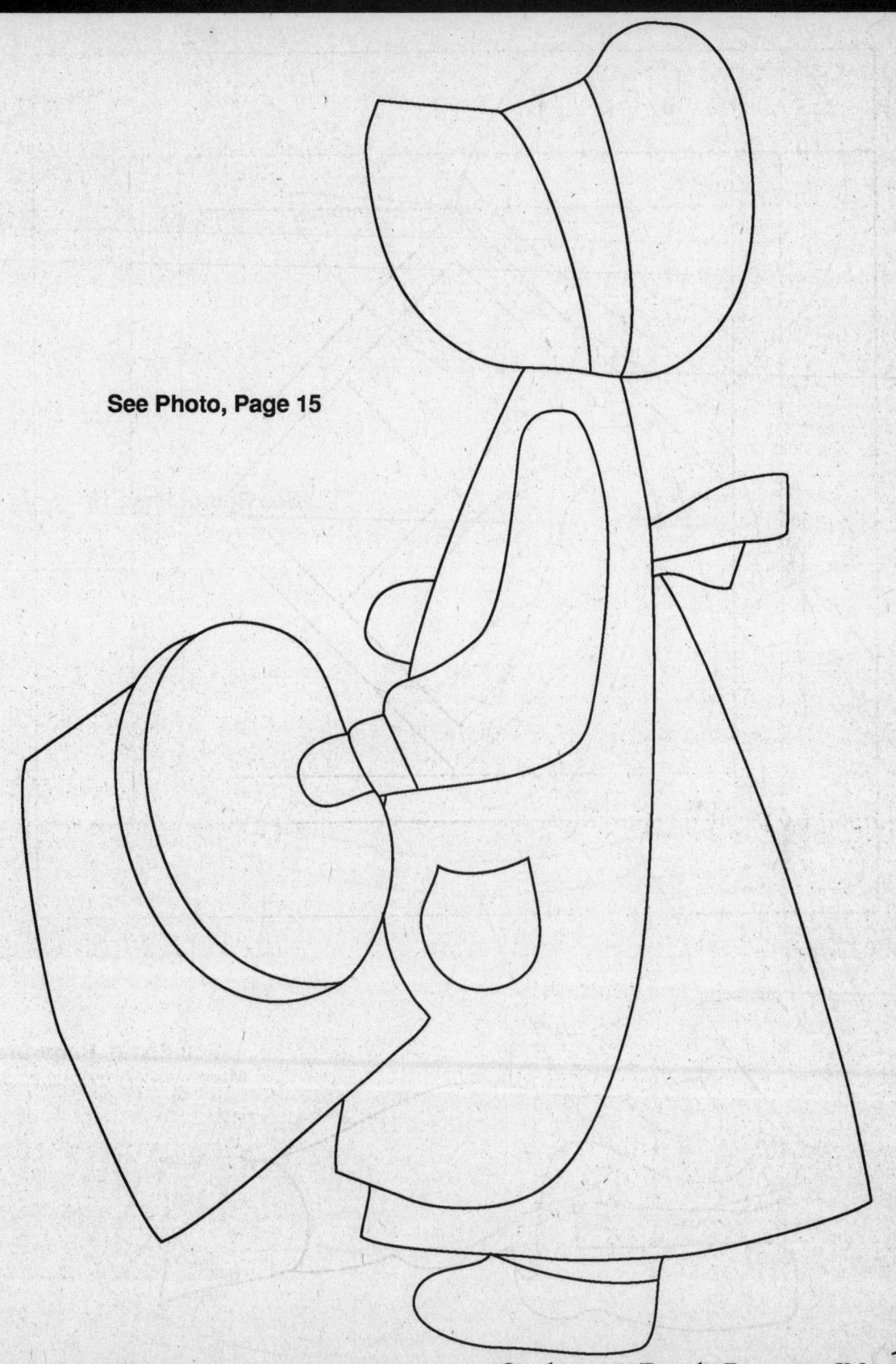

See Photo, Page 15

Sunbonnet FAMILY REUNION

Me
Victorena Stanis • Westville, IL

See Photo, Page 15

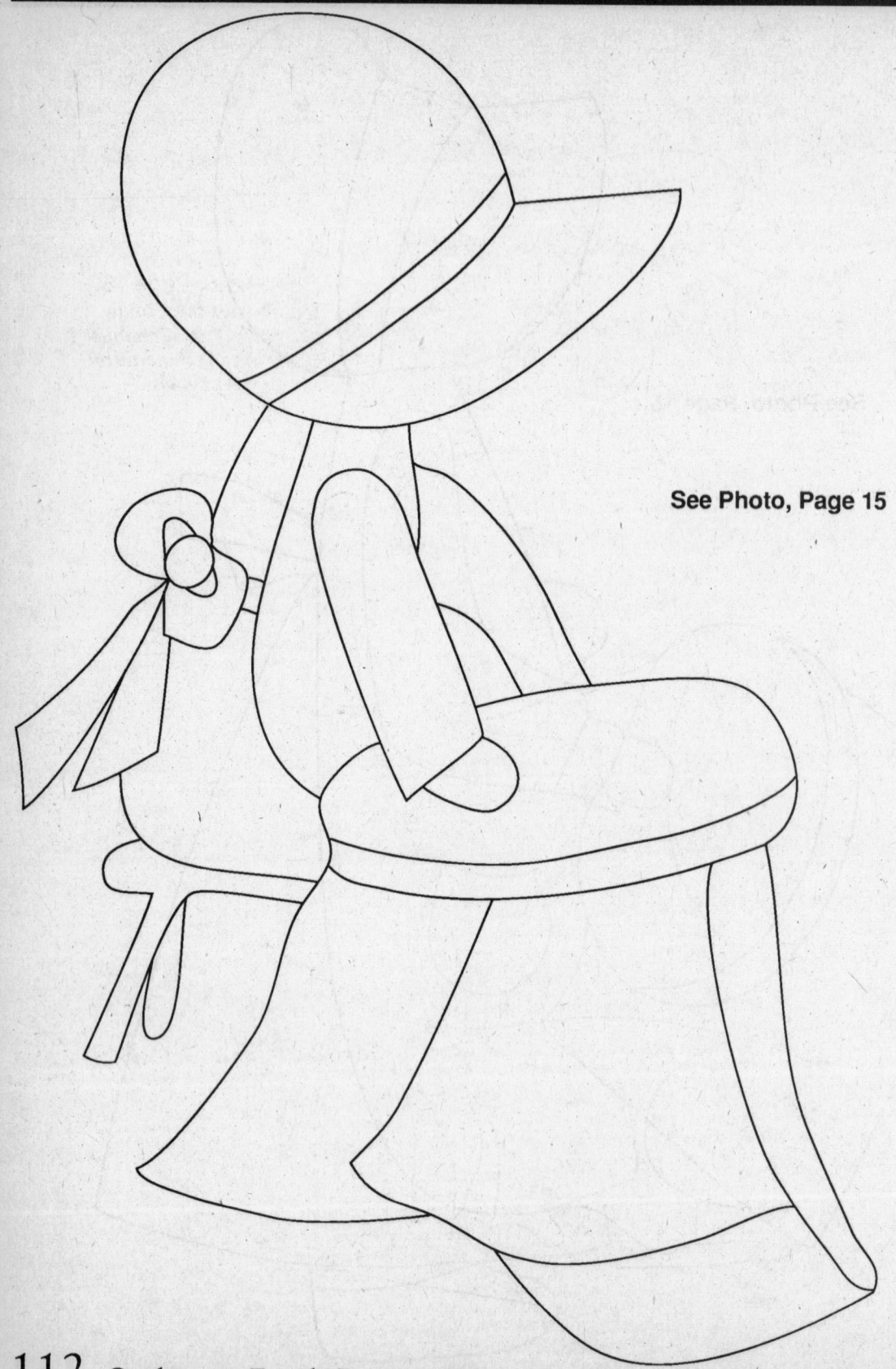

Sunbonnet Family Reunion IV

Christel Cowgirl
Sandra Andrews • Medina, OH

Sunbonnet FAMILY REUNION

See Photo, Page 16
Match with next page.
Taken from *The Sunbonnet Family of Quilt Patterns* by Dolores Hinson.

Sunbonnet Family Reunion IV 113

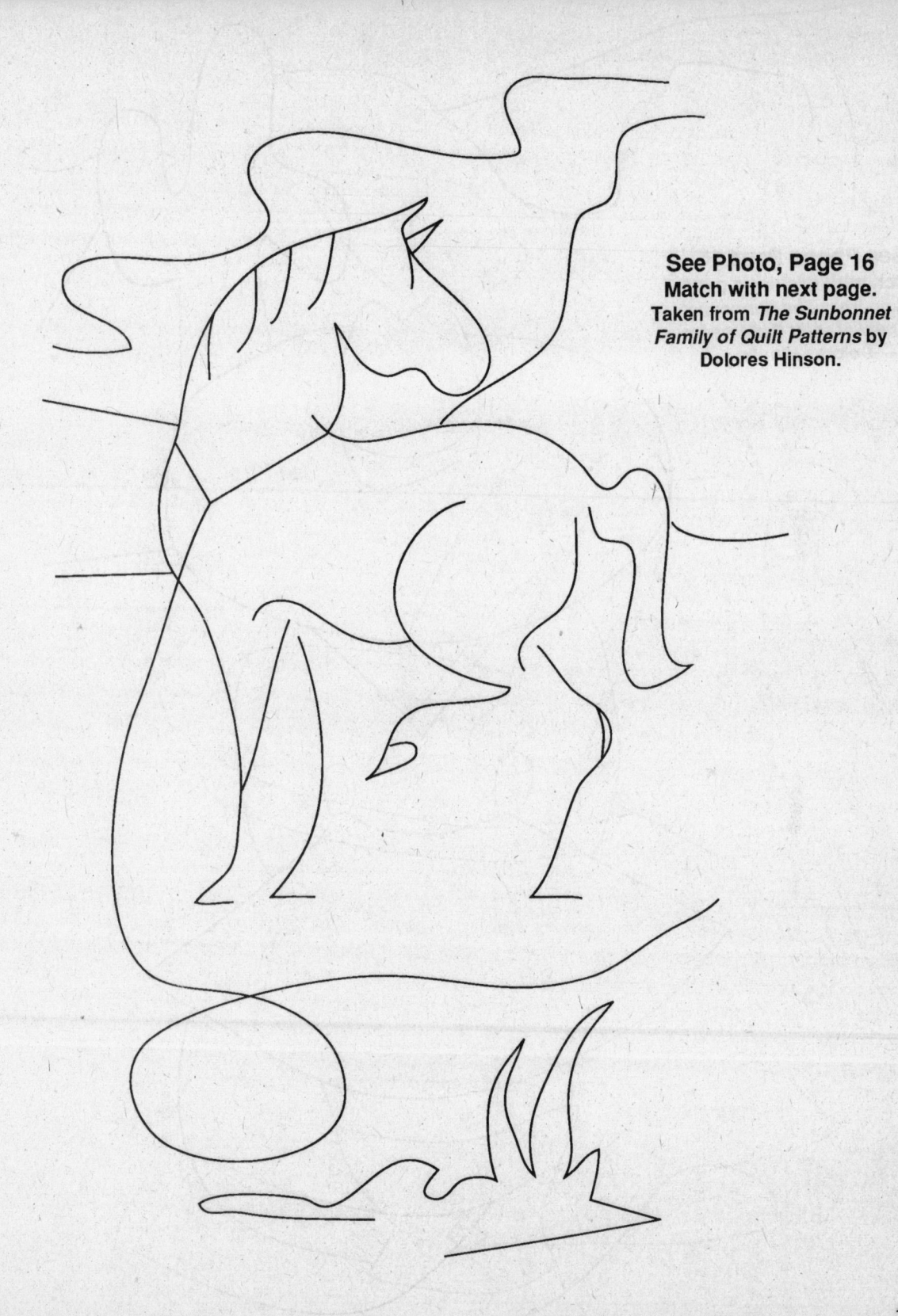

Sunbonnet
FAMILY REUNION

See Photo, Page 16
Match with previous page.
Taken from *The Sunbonnet Family of Quilt Patterns* by Dolores Hinson.

114   Sunbonnet Family Reunion IV

School Days
Jean Klepinger • Greenville, OH

Sunbonnet FAMILY REUNION

See Photo, Page 16

Sunbonnet Family Reunion IV

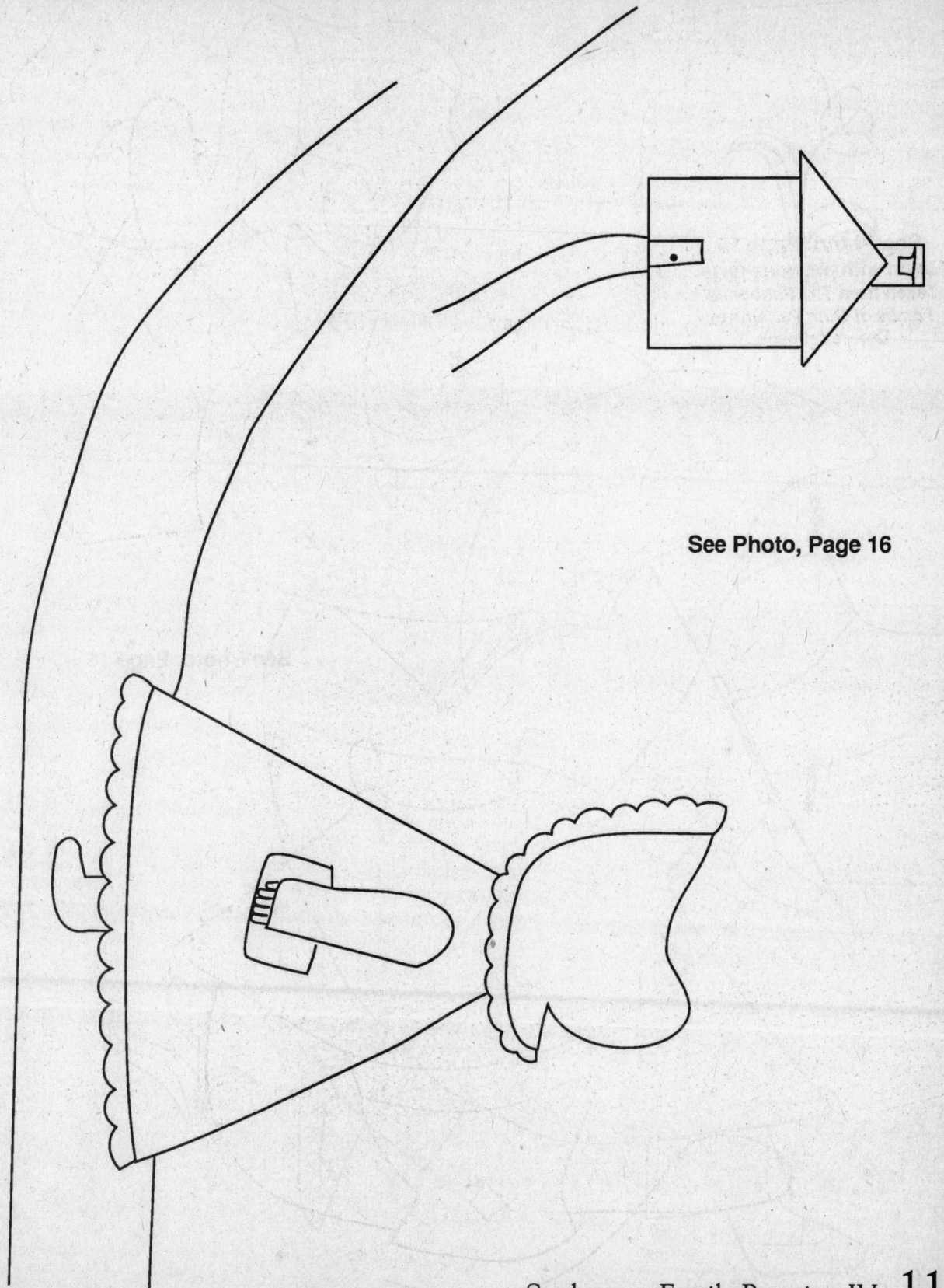

Sunbonnet FAMILY REUNION

Rainy Day Sue
Hannah Ames • Harvard, IL

See Photo, Page 16

116 Sunbonnet Family Reunion IV

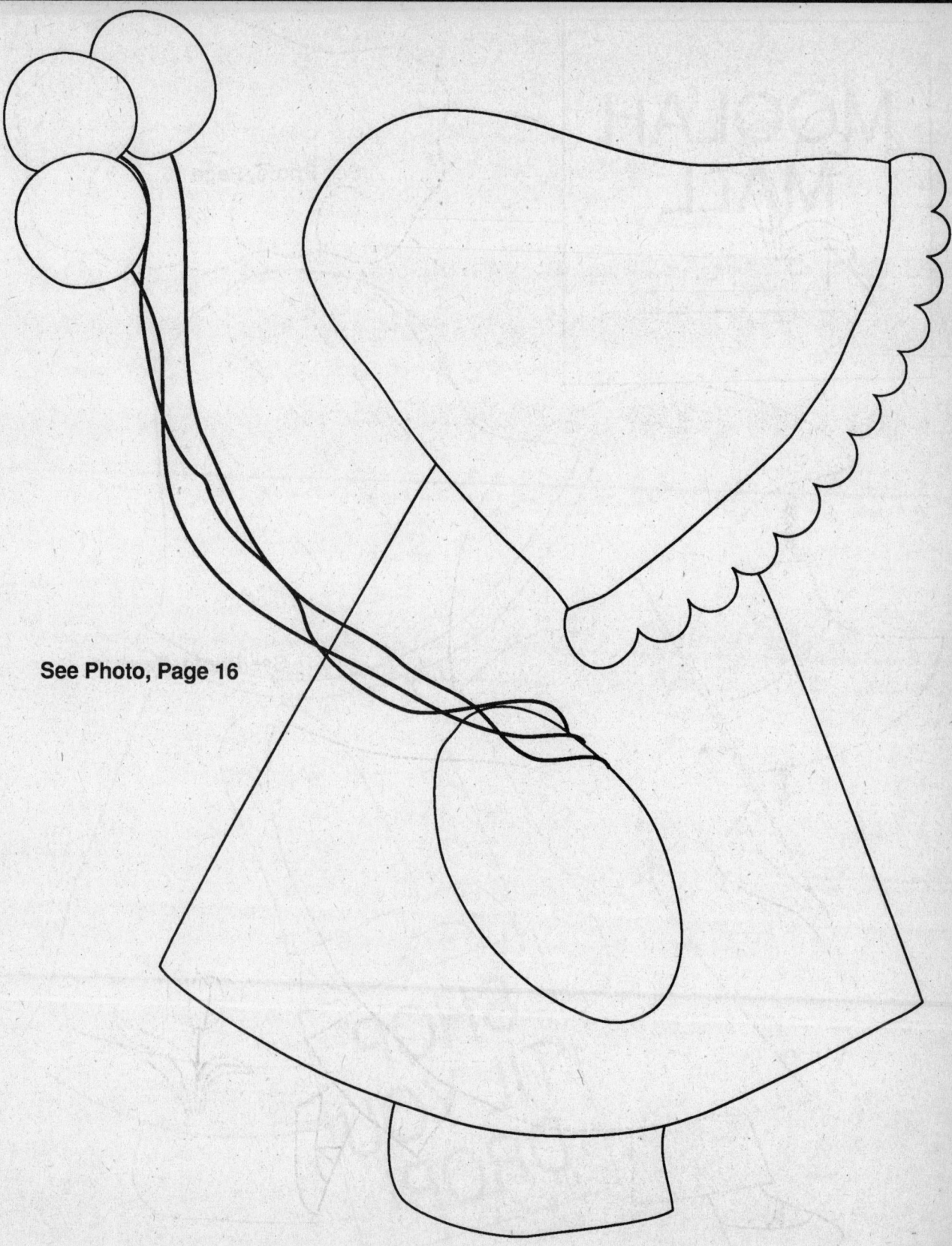

Lil Miss Sunbonnet
Melba F. Mitchell • Stanton, CA

See Photo, Page 16

Sunbonnet Family Reunion IV 117

Sunbonnet FAMILY REUNION

More Fabric
Virginia Caudell • Wynne, AR

MOOLAH MALL ←

See Photo, Page 16

SHOP 'TIL YOU DROP!

118 Sunbonnet Family Reunion IV

Walking & Camping
Sharon Larson • The Colony, TX

Sunbonnet FAMILY REUNION

See Photo, Page 16

Sunbonnet Family Reunion IV 119

Sunbonnet FAMILY REUNION

Sue In The Garden
Carol Deal • Bloomington, IL

See Photo, Page 16

120 Sunbonnet Family Reunion IV

Sunbonnet Sue 10K
Linda King-Johnson • Barryville, NY

Sunbonnet FAMILY REUNION

SUNBONNET SUE 10K

See Photo, Page 16
Match with next page.

Sunbonnet Family Reunion IV 121

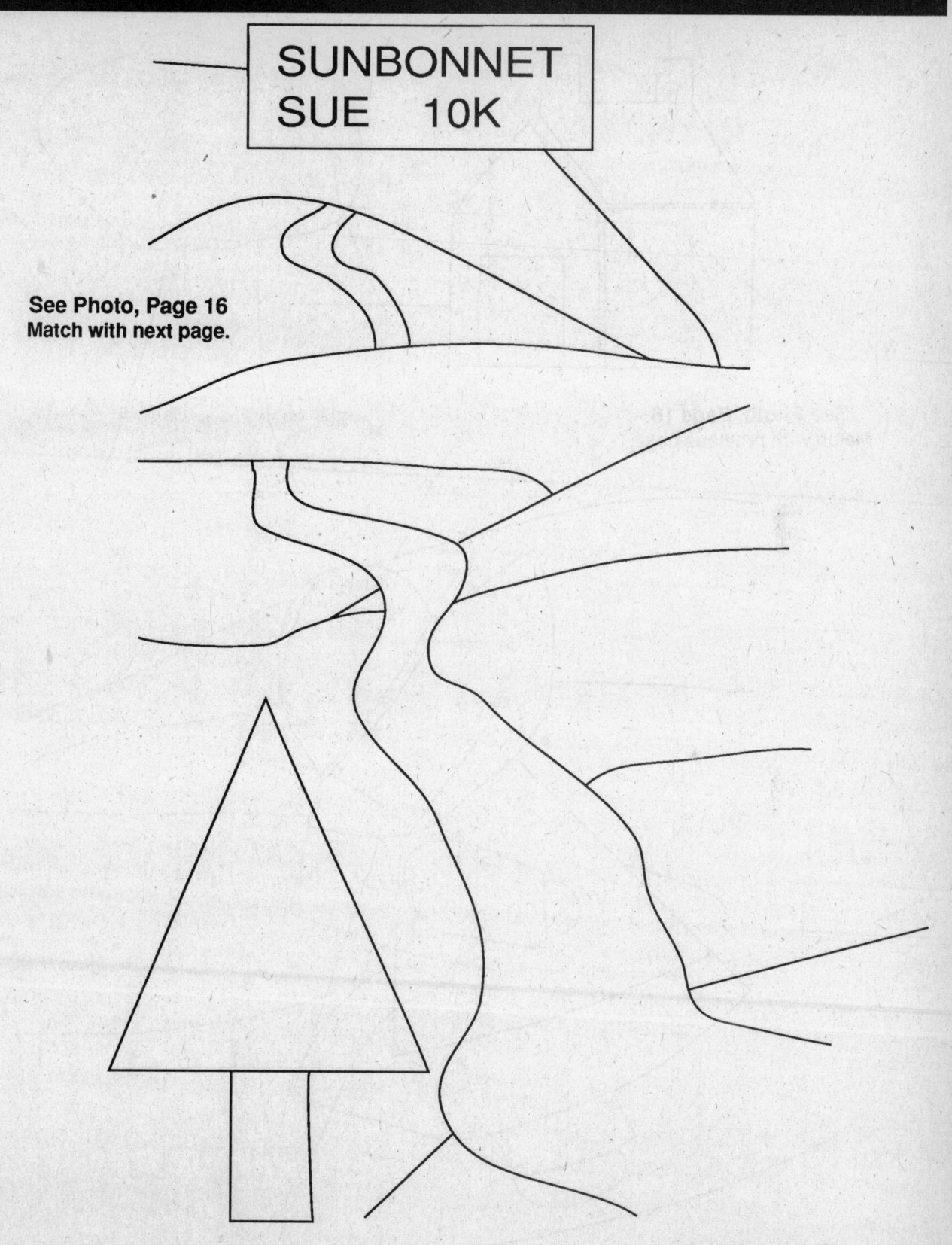

Sunbonnet
FAMILY REUNION

See Photo, Page 16
Match with previous page.

122 Sunbonnet Family Reunion IV

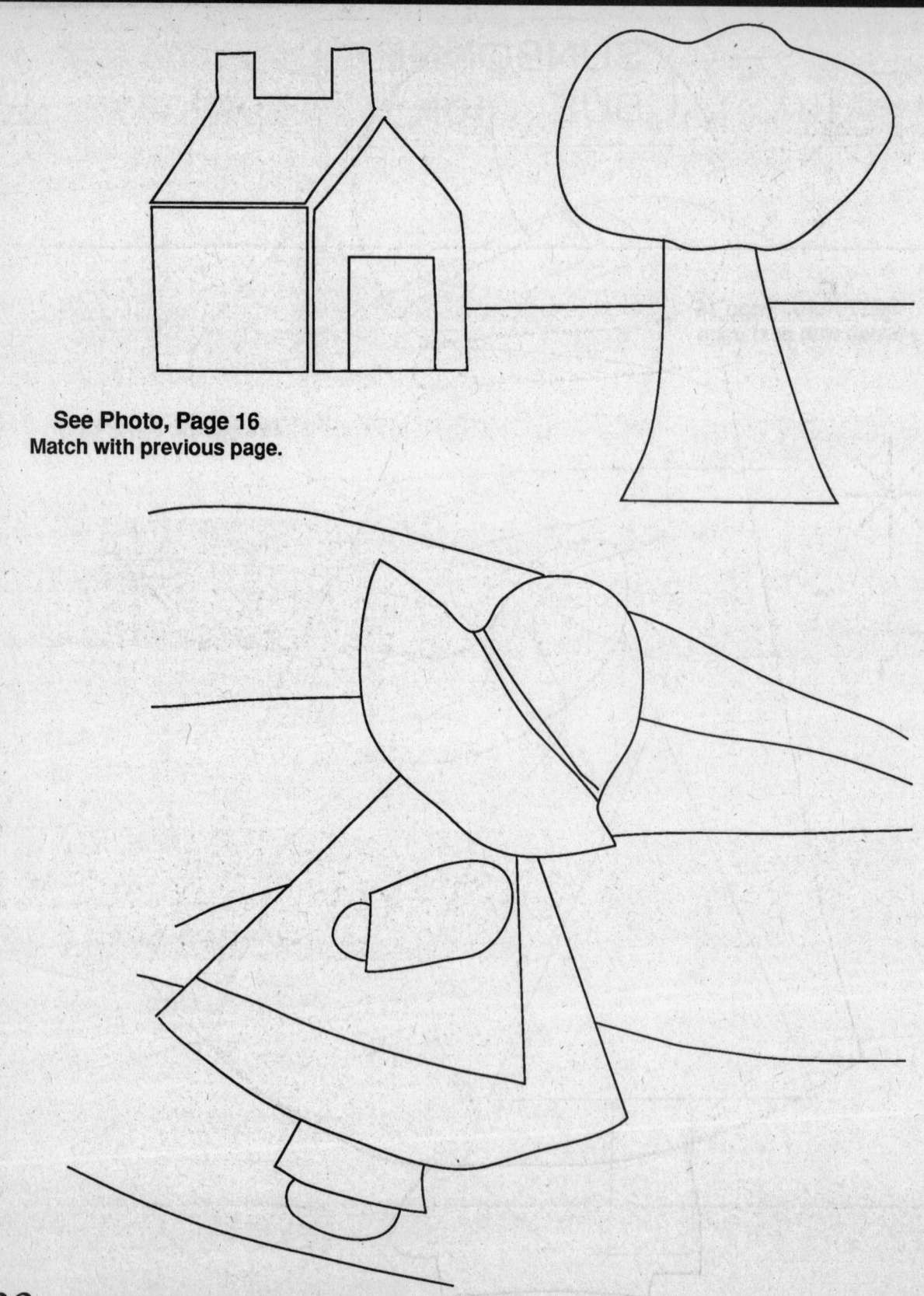

Star Light, Star Bright
Teresa Richard • New York Mills, NY

Sunbonnet FAMILY REUNION

See Photo, Page 16

Sunbonnet Family Reunion IV 123

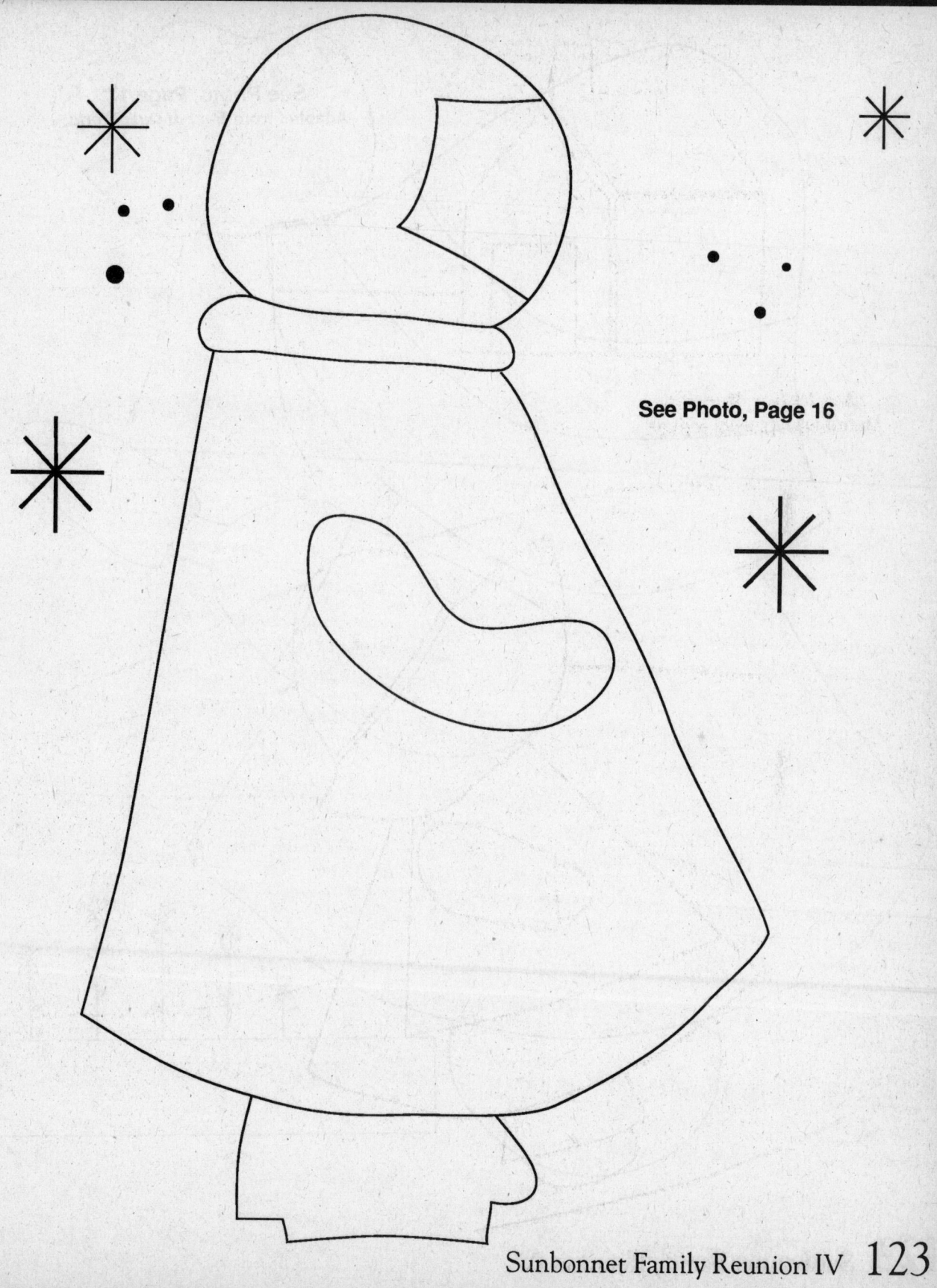

Sunbonnet FAMILY REUNION

The Garden
Jane Allen • Tipp City, OH

See Photo, Page 17
Adapted from *Best of Quilt World*.

124 Sunbonnet Family Reunion IV

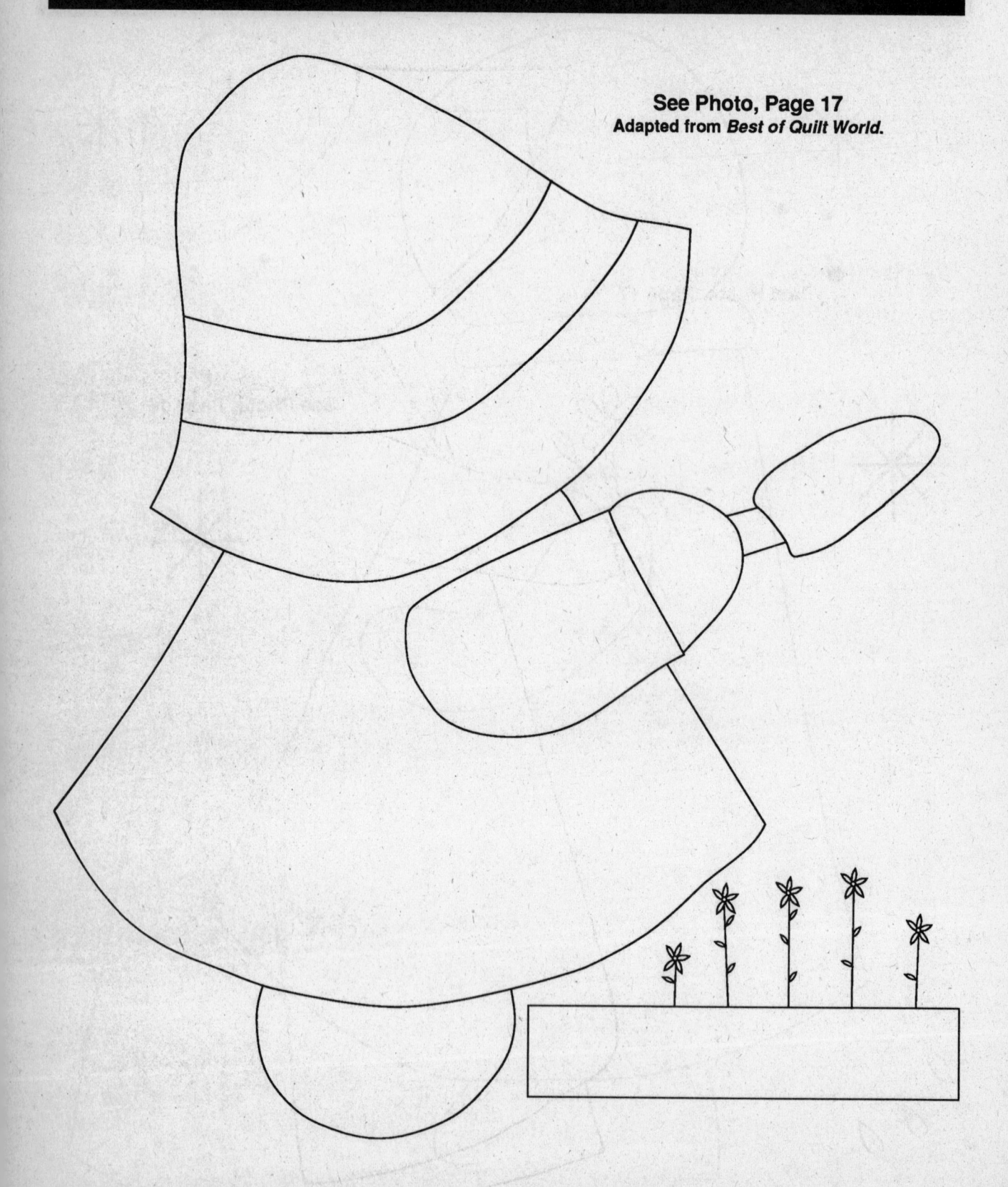

He Loves Me!
Patricia Yerks • Pine Bush, NY

See Photo, Page 17

Sunbonnet Family Reunion IV

Sunbonnet FAMILY REUNION

Amish Flowers
Christine Tucker • Kailua, HI

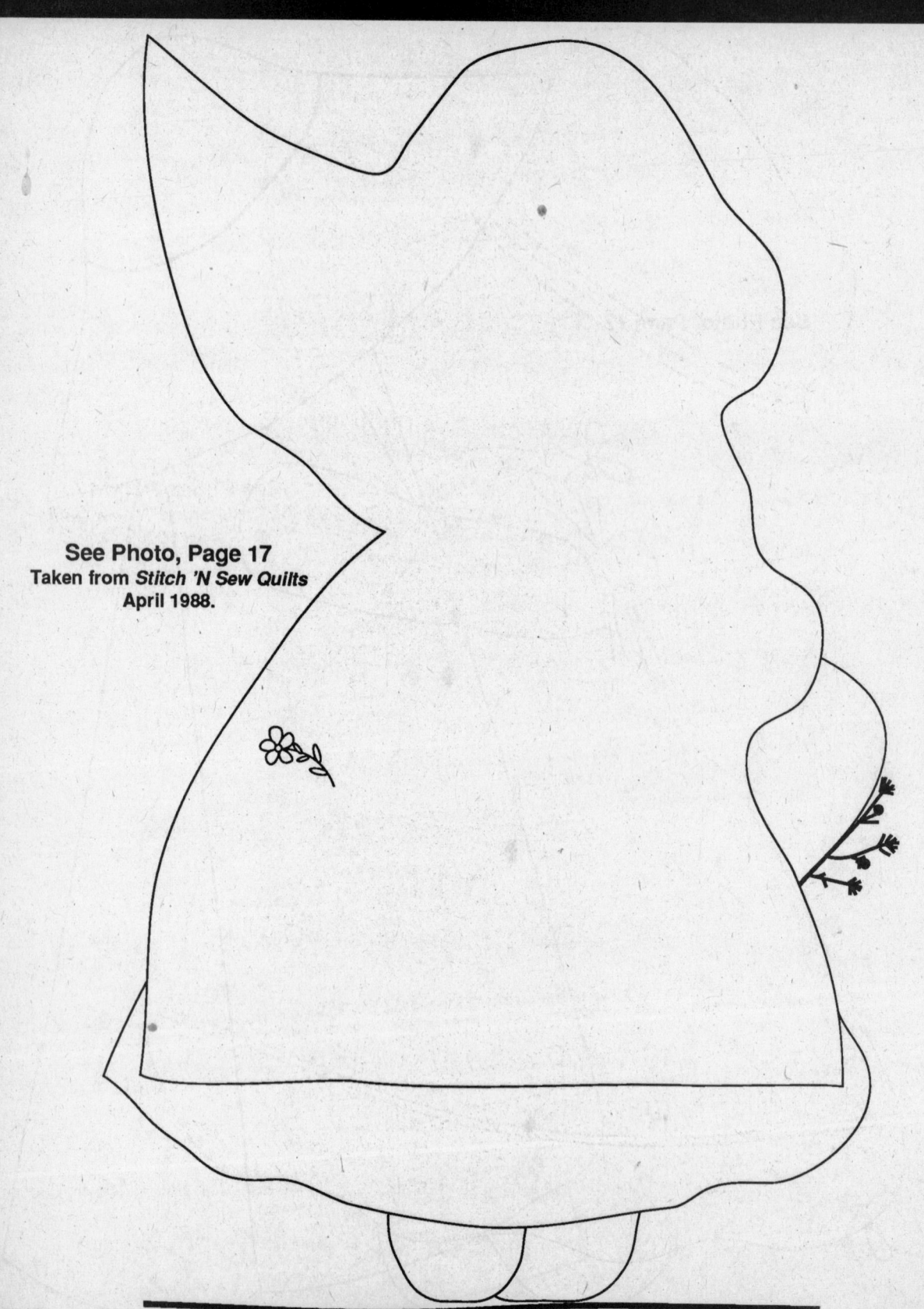

See Photo, Page 17
Taken from *Stitch 'N Sew Quilts* April 1988.

126 Sunbonnet Family Reunion IV

Shy Sunbonnet
Joan Shook • Tombstone, AZ

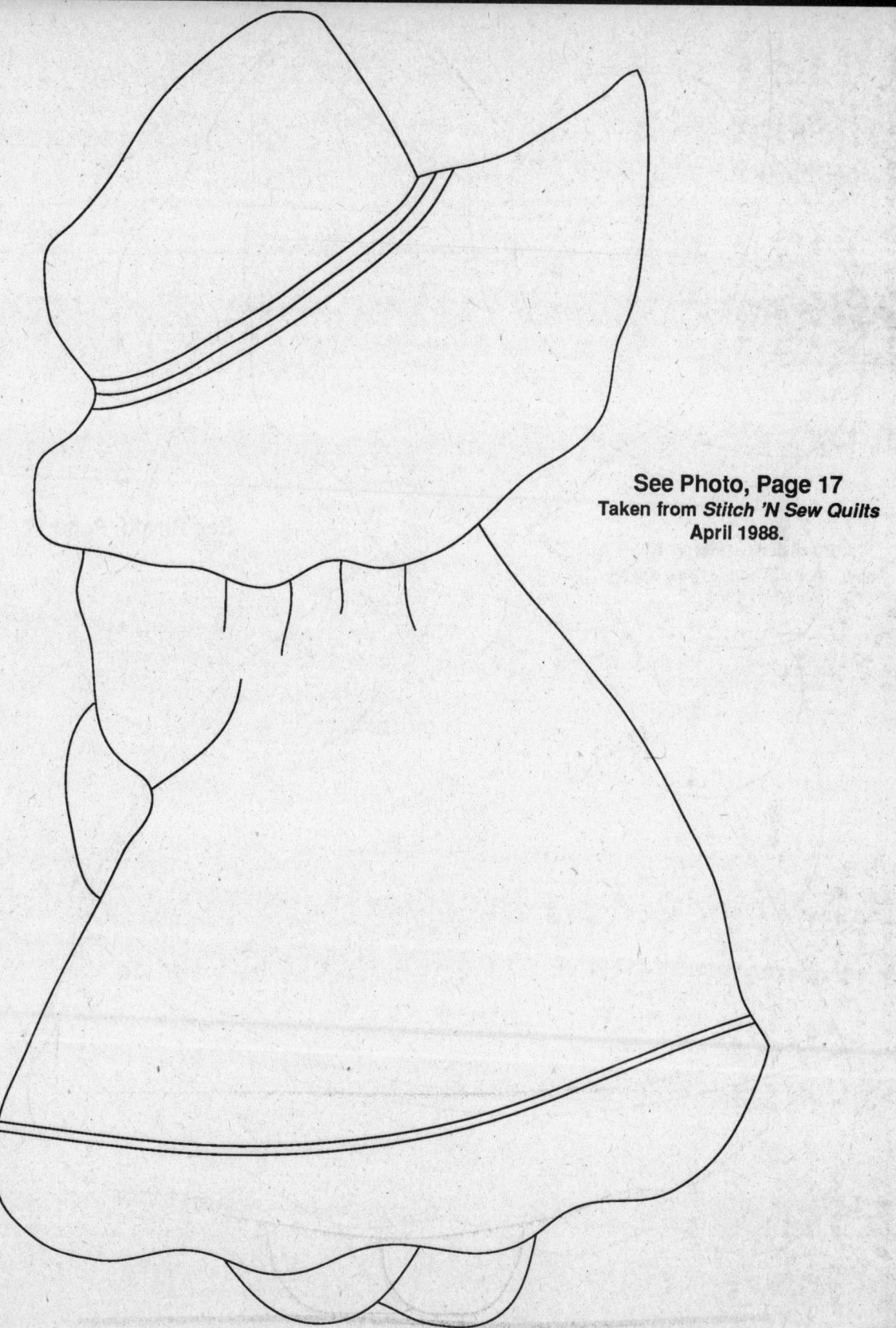

See Photo, Page 17
Taken from *Stitch 'N Sew Quilts*
April 1988.

Sunbonnet Family Reunion IV

Sunbonnet FAMILY REUNION

Sue In Pink
Mickey Singer • Pittsburgh, PA

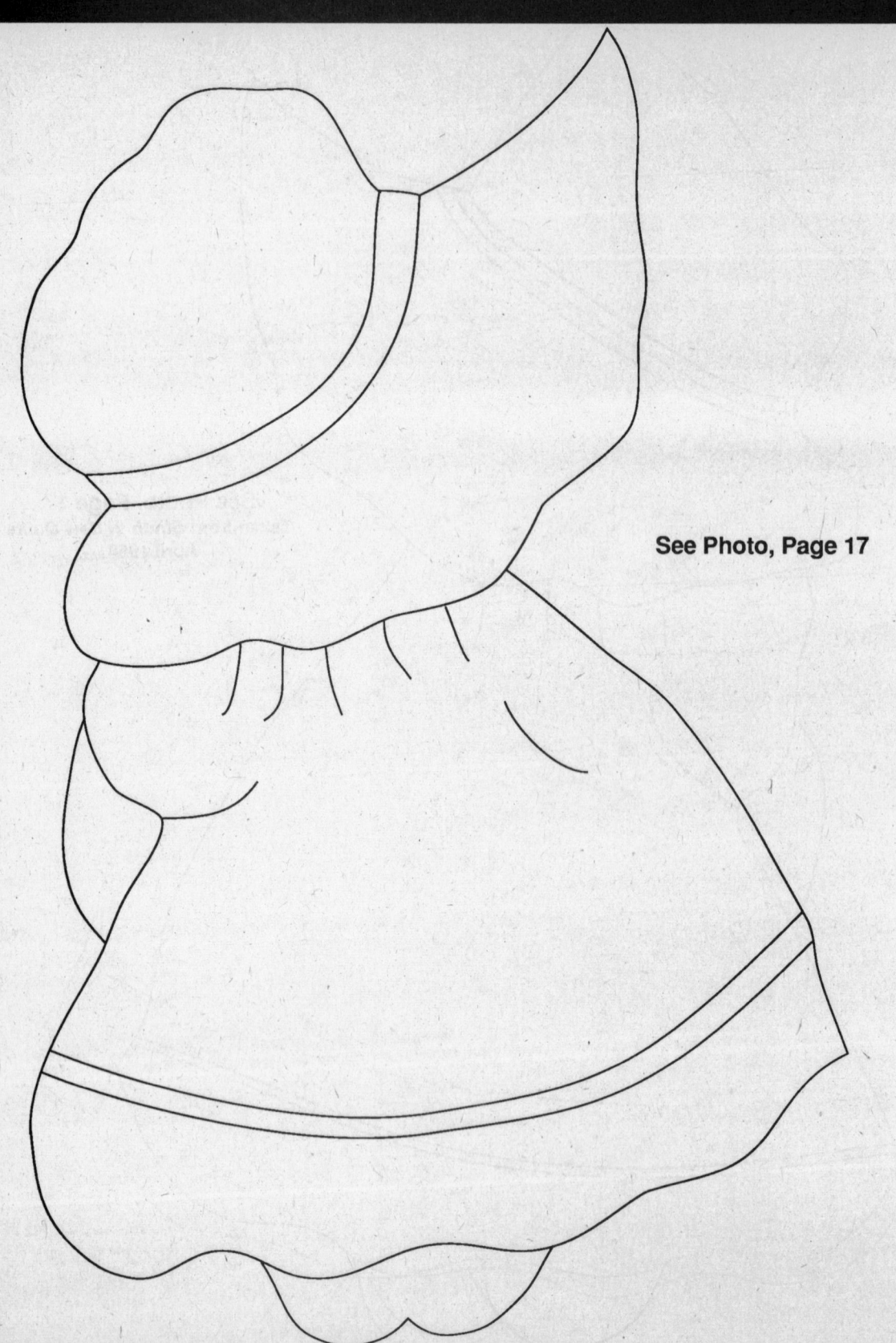

See Photo, Page 17

128 Sunbonnet Family Reunion IV

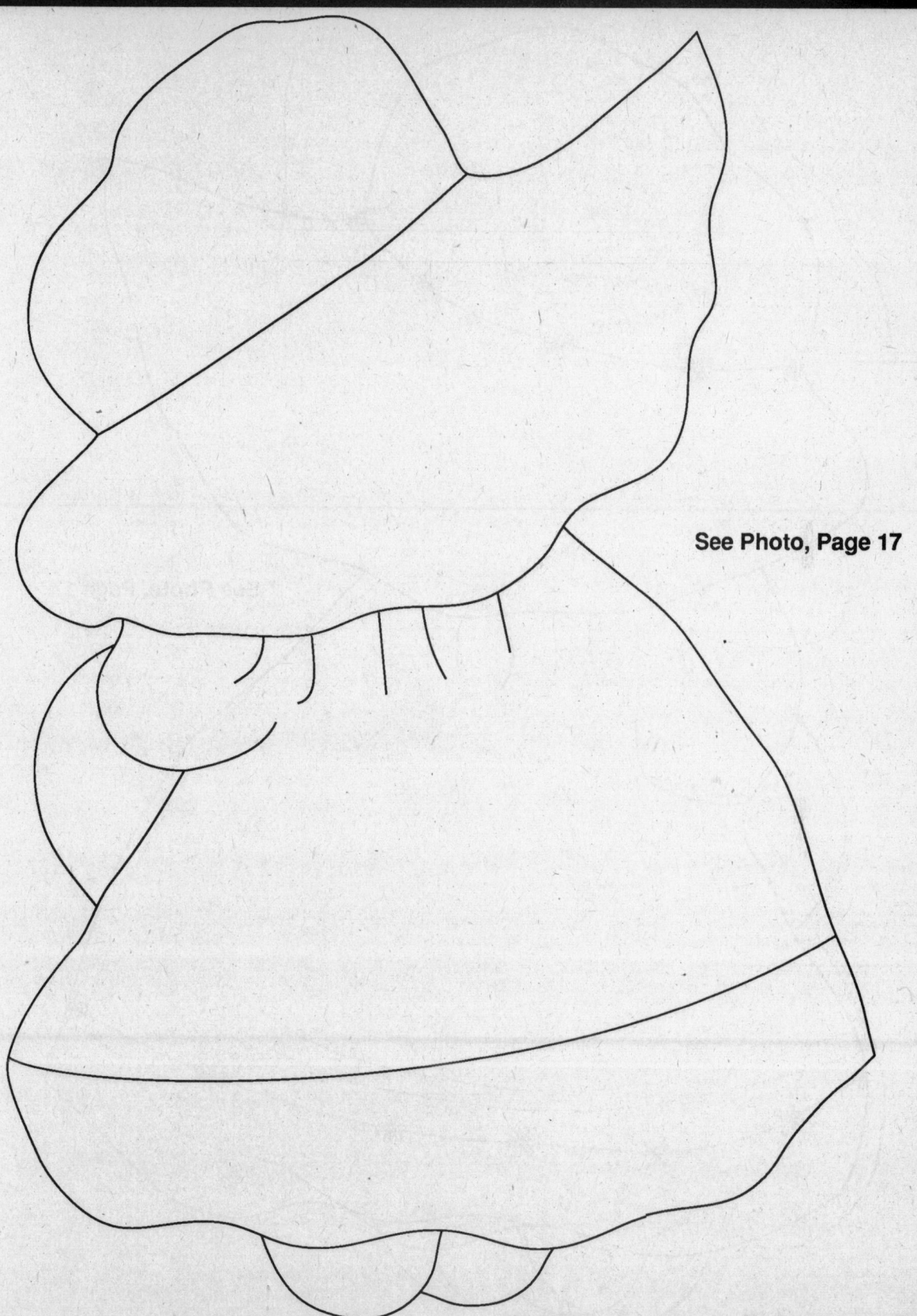

Sunbonnet Baby
Ruth Carroll • Patterson, VA

Sunbonnet FAMILY REUNION

See Photo, Page 17

Sunbonnet Family Reunion IV 129

Sunbonnet FAMILY REUNION

Lookin' Pretty
Janet L. Parsons • Monaca, PA

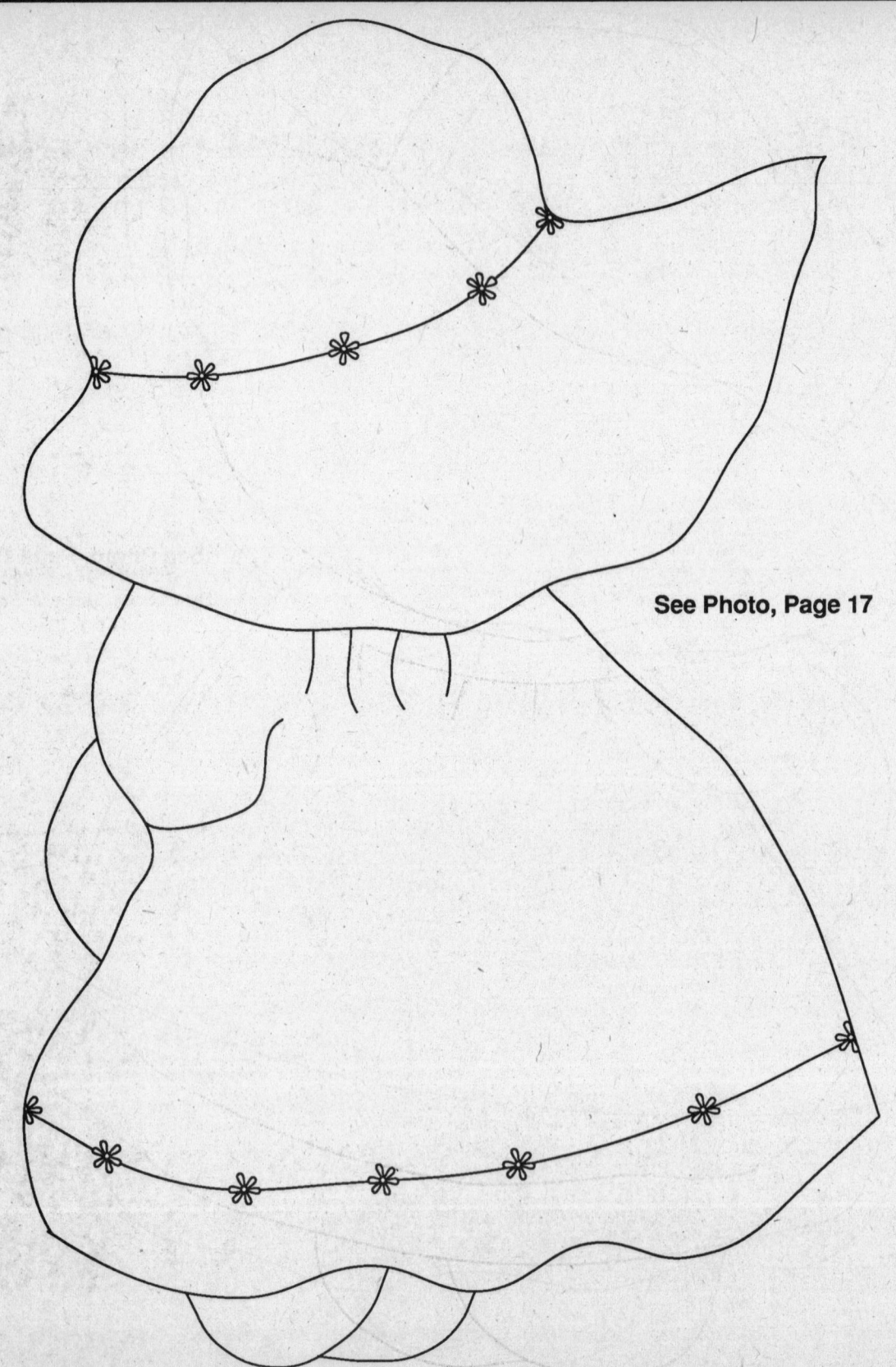

See Photo, Page 17

130 Sunbonnet Family Reunion IV

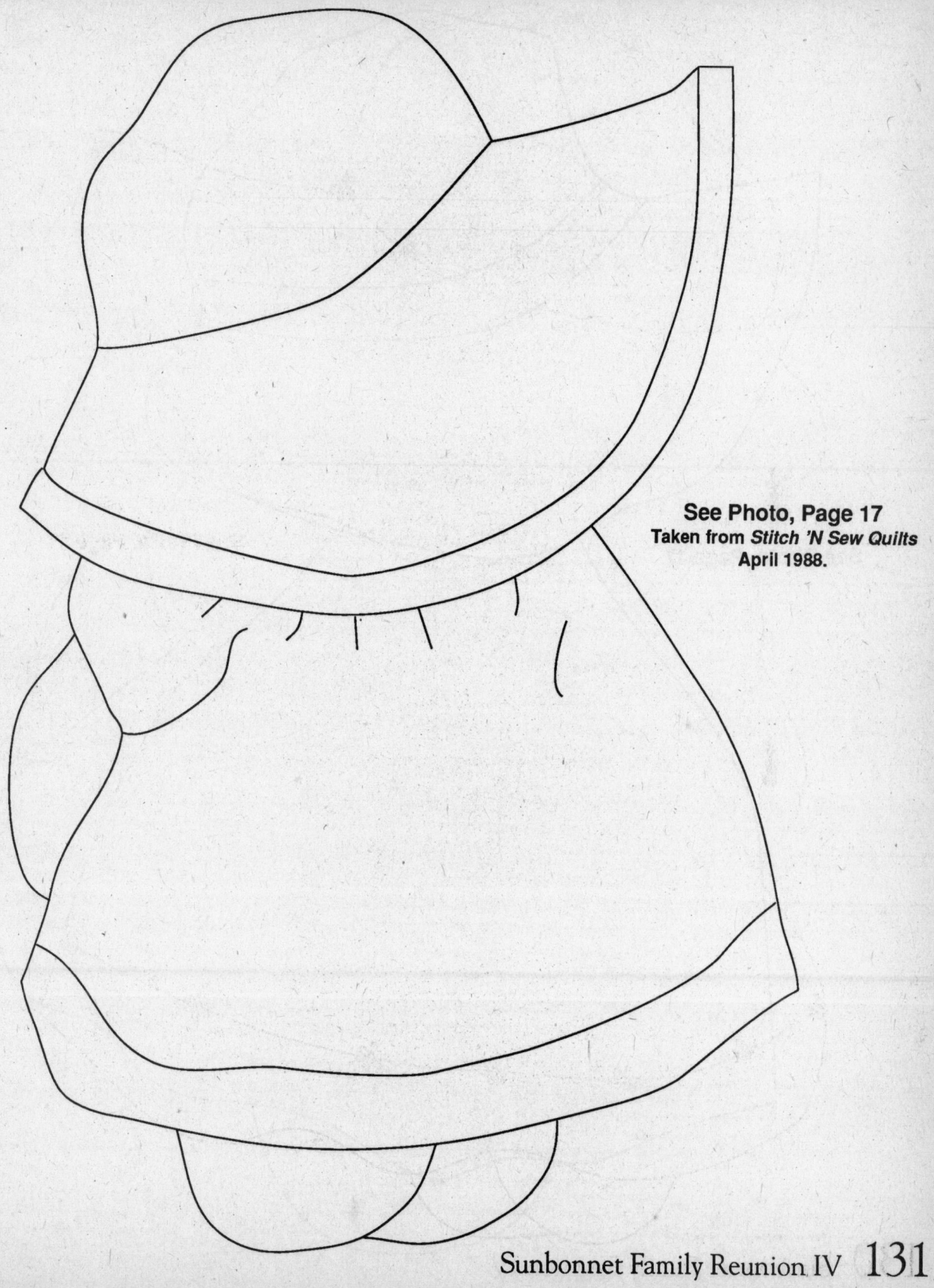

Sunbonnet Baby
Mary Lewis • Locust Grove, OK

Sunbonnet FAMILY REUNION

See Photo, Page 17
Taken from *Stitch 'N Sew Quilts*
April 1988.

Sunbonnet Family Reunion IV

Sunbonnet Baby & Her Frog
Cinthia Lou Stolte • McLouth, KS

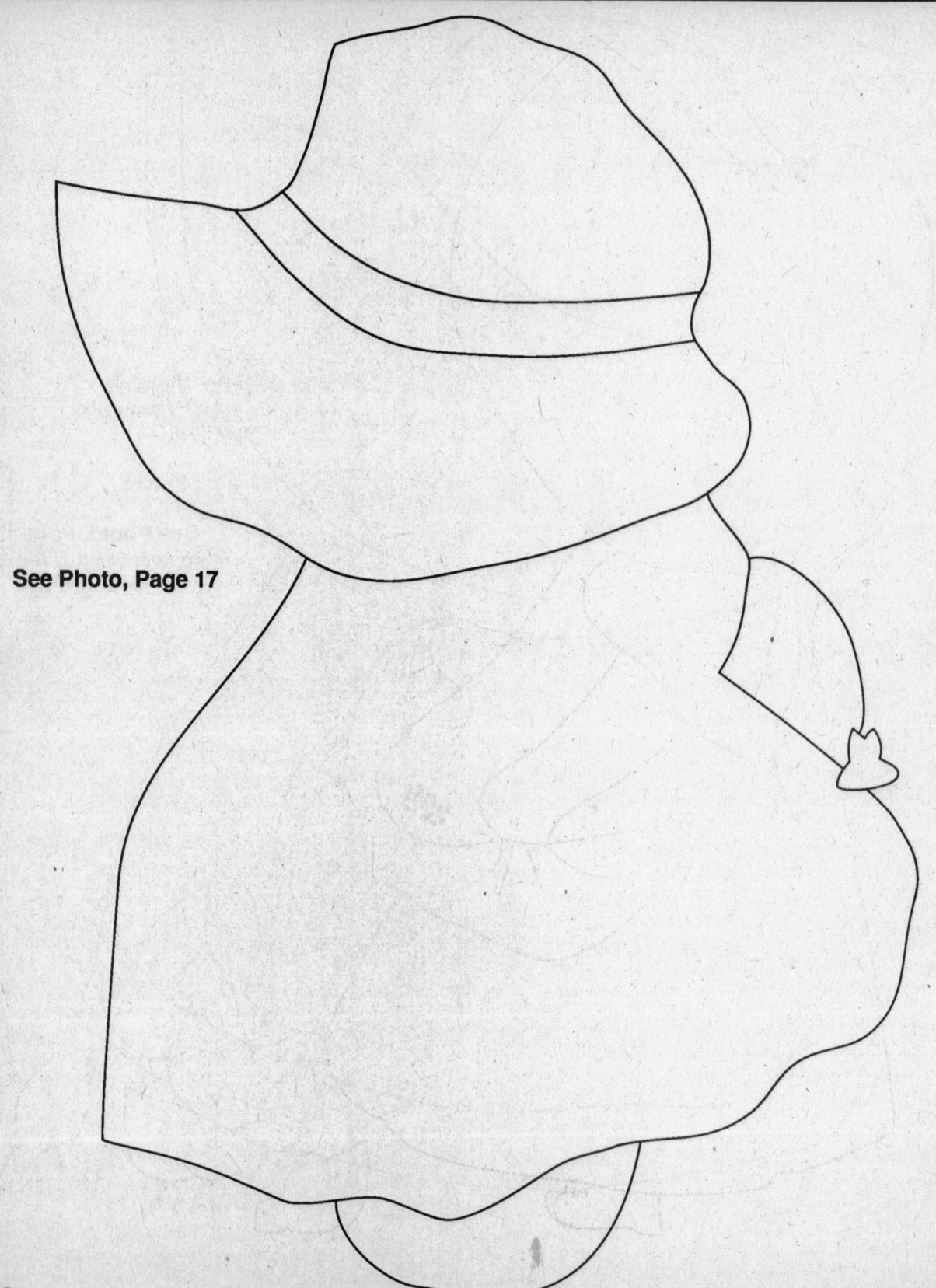

See Photo, Page 17

132 Sunbonnet Family Reunion IV

Feeding Time
Georgia Engle • E. Helena, MT

Sunbonnet FAMILY REUNION

See Photo, Page 18
Taken from *Stitch 'N Sew Quilts*
April 1988.

Sunbonnet FAMILY REUNION

My Calm In The Chaos
Sherry L. McConnell • Anderson, IN

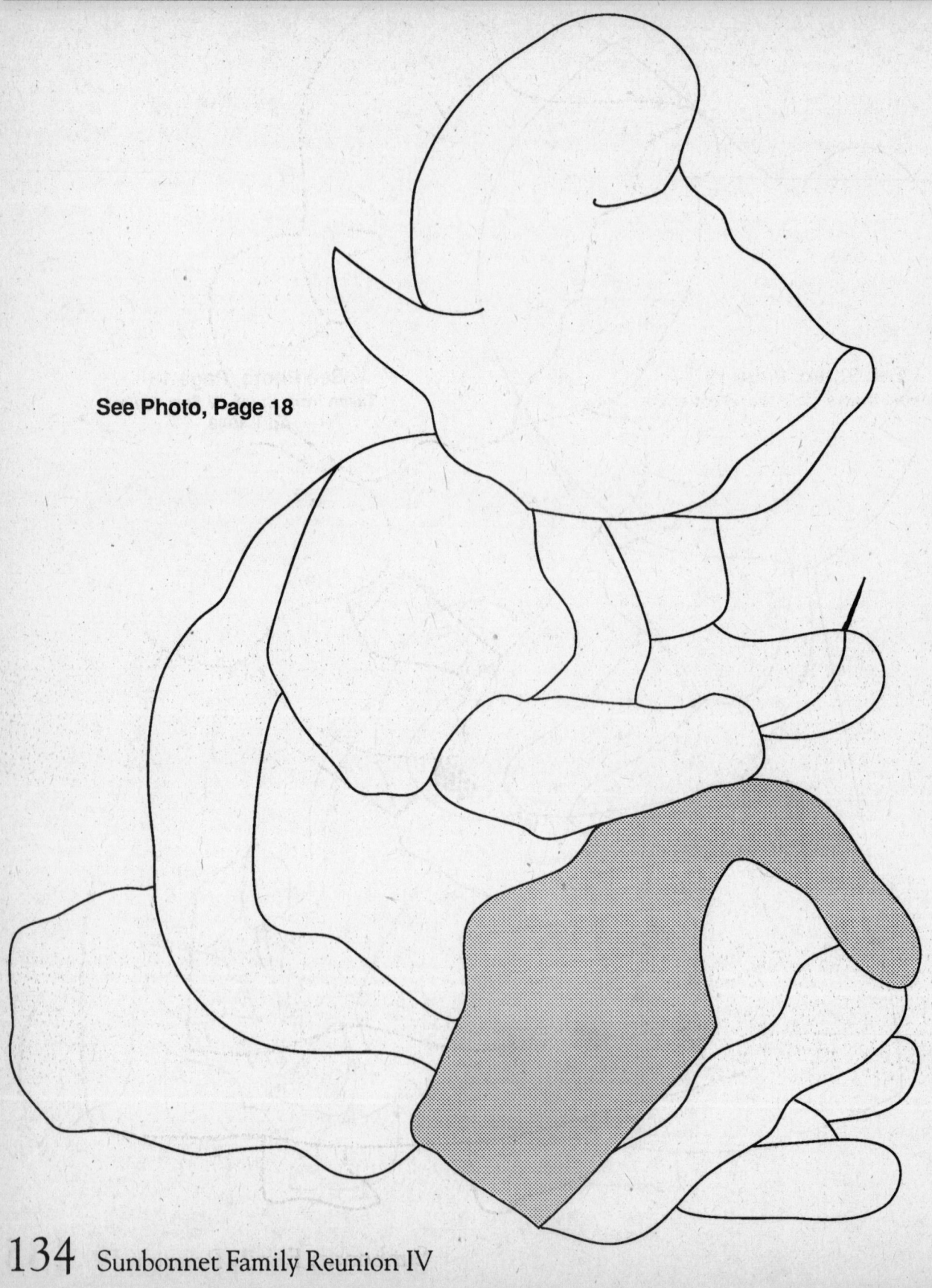

See Photo, Page 18

134 Sunbonnet Family Reunion IV

Sunbonnet Sue With Quilt Book
Betty Dunlap • Kansas City, MO

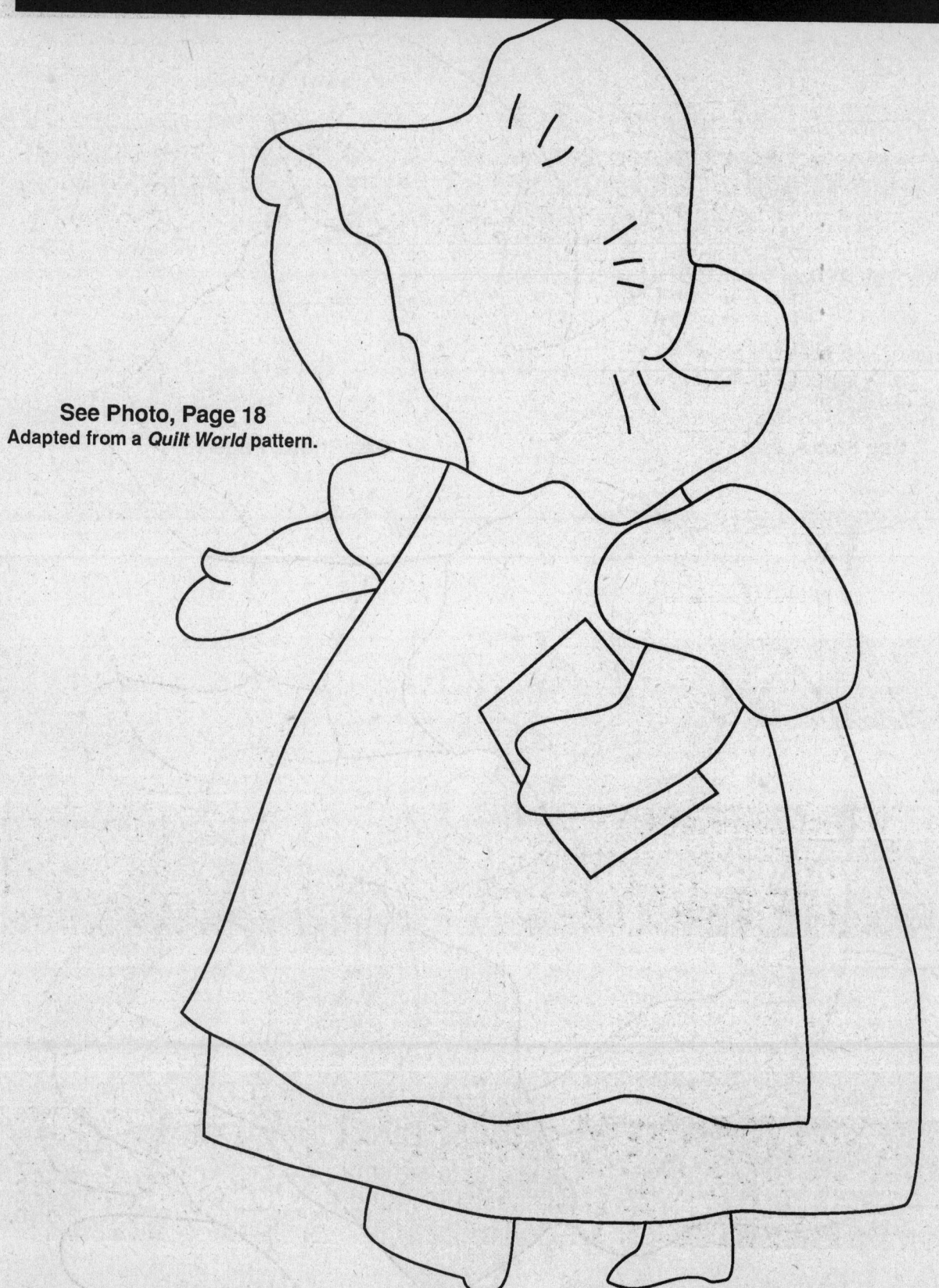

See Photo, Page 18
Adapted from a *Quilt World* pattern.

Sunbonnet Family Reunion IV

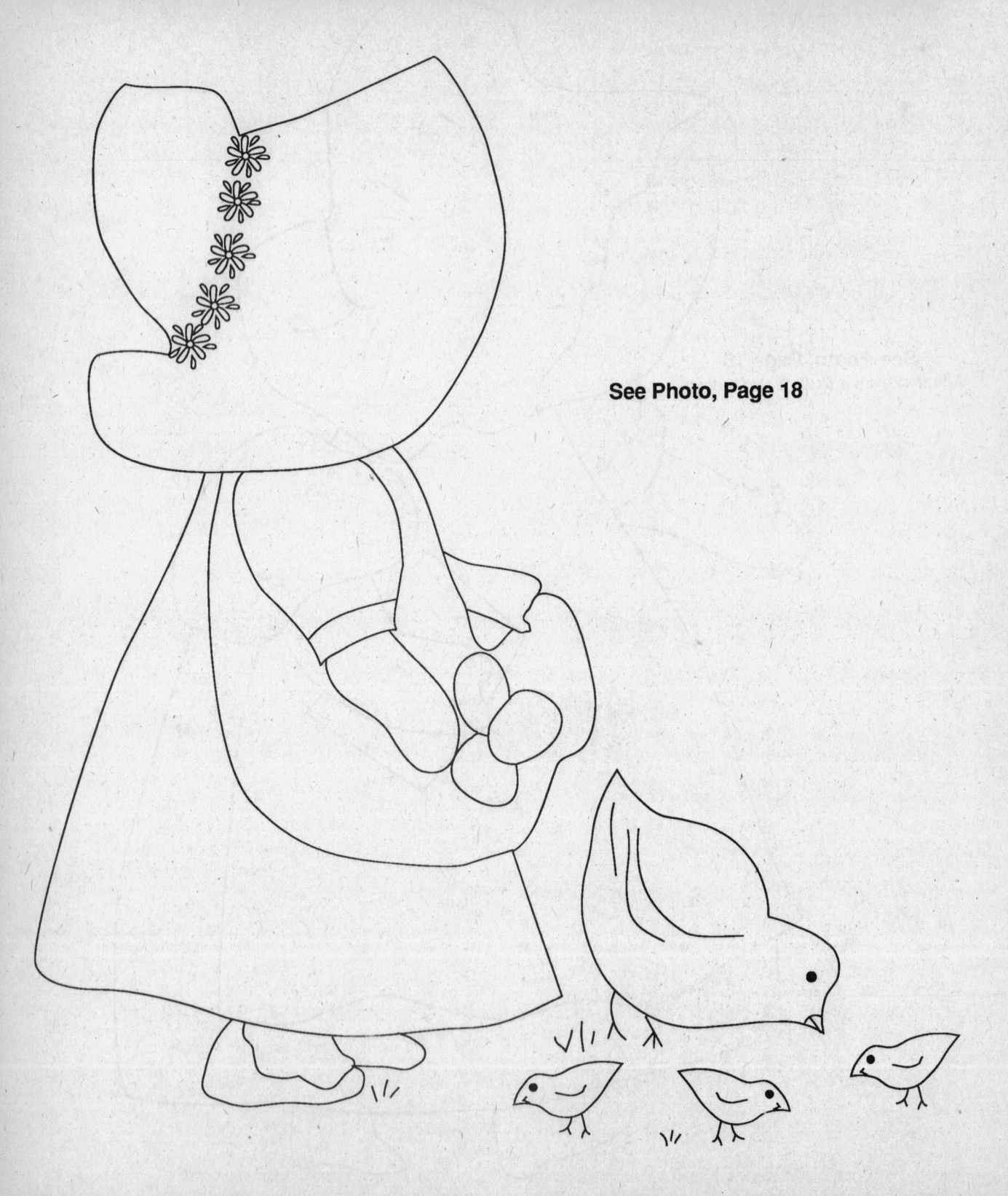

Sunbonnet FAMILY REUNION

Gathering Eggs
Laura M. Ramseier • Oshkosh, WI

See Photo, Page 18

Picnic Friends
Tami Shoji • Chatham, Ont., Canada

Sunbonnet FAMILY REUNION

See Photo, Page 18
Match with next page.

Sunbonnet Family Reunion IV 137

Sunbonnet FAMILY REUNION

See Photo, Page 18
Match with previous page.

138 Sunbonnet Family Reunion IV

Mary Christmas 1911
Dorothy Brock • Helena, MT

Sunbonnet FAMILY REUNION

See Photo, Page 18
Taken from *The Sunbonnet Family of Quilt Patterns* by Dolores Hinson.

Sunbonnet Family Reunion IV

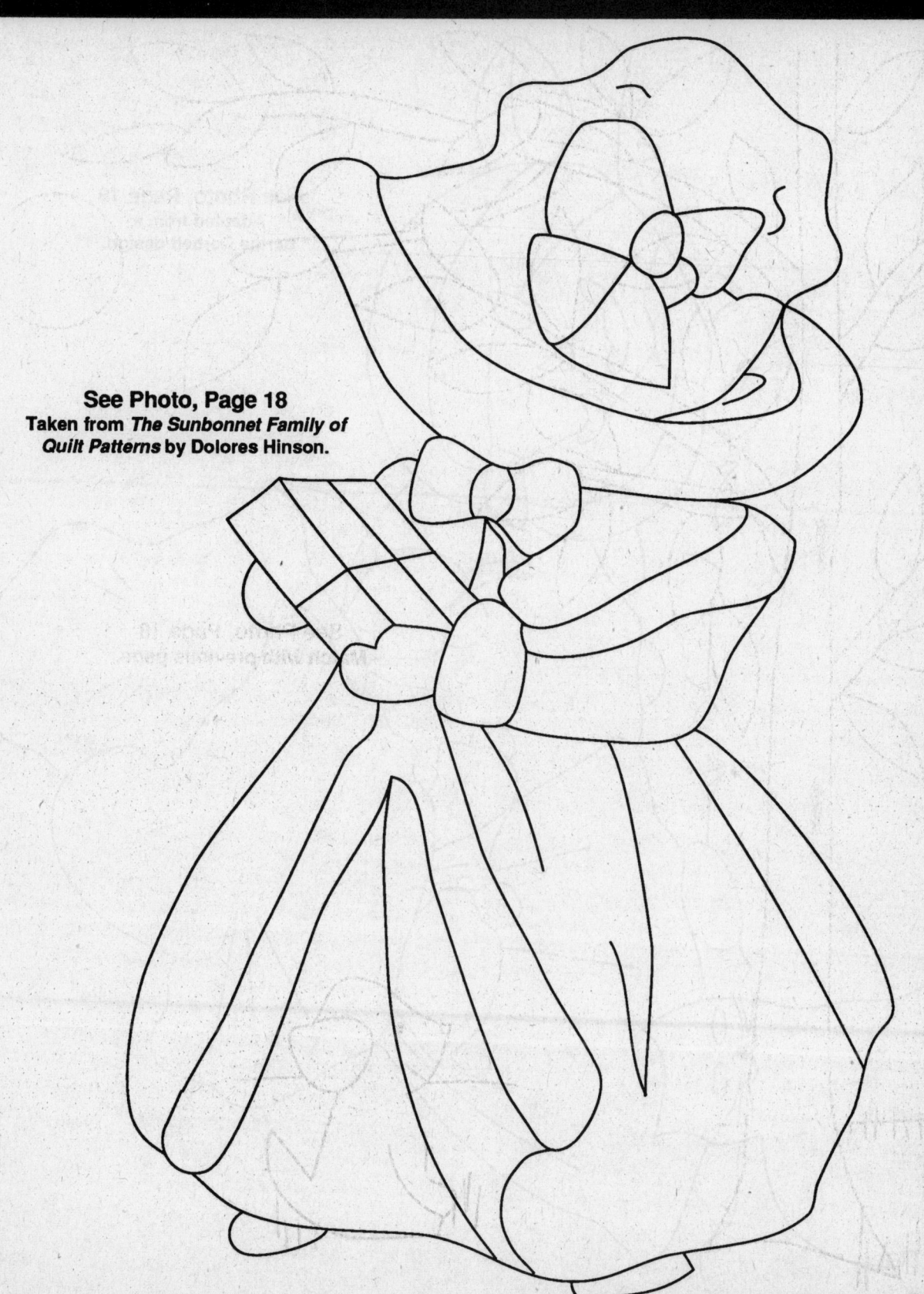

Sunbonnet FAMILY REUNION

Trick Or Treat
Kit D. Carpenter • Greenwell Springs, LA

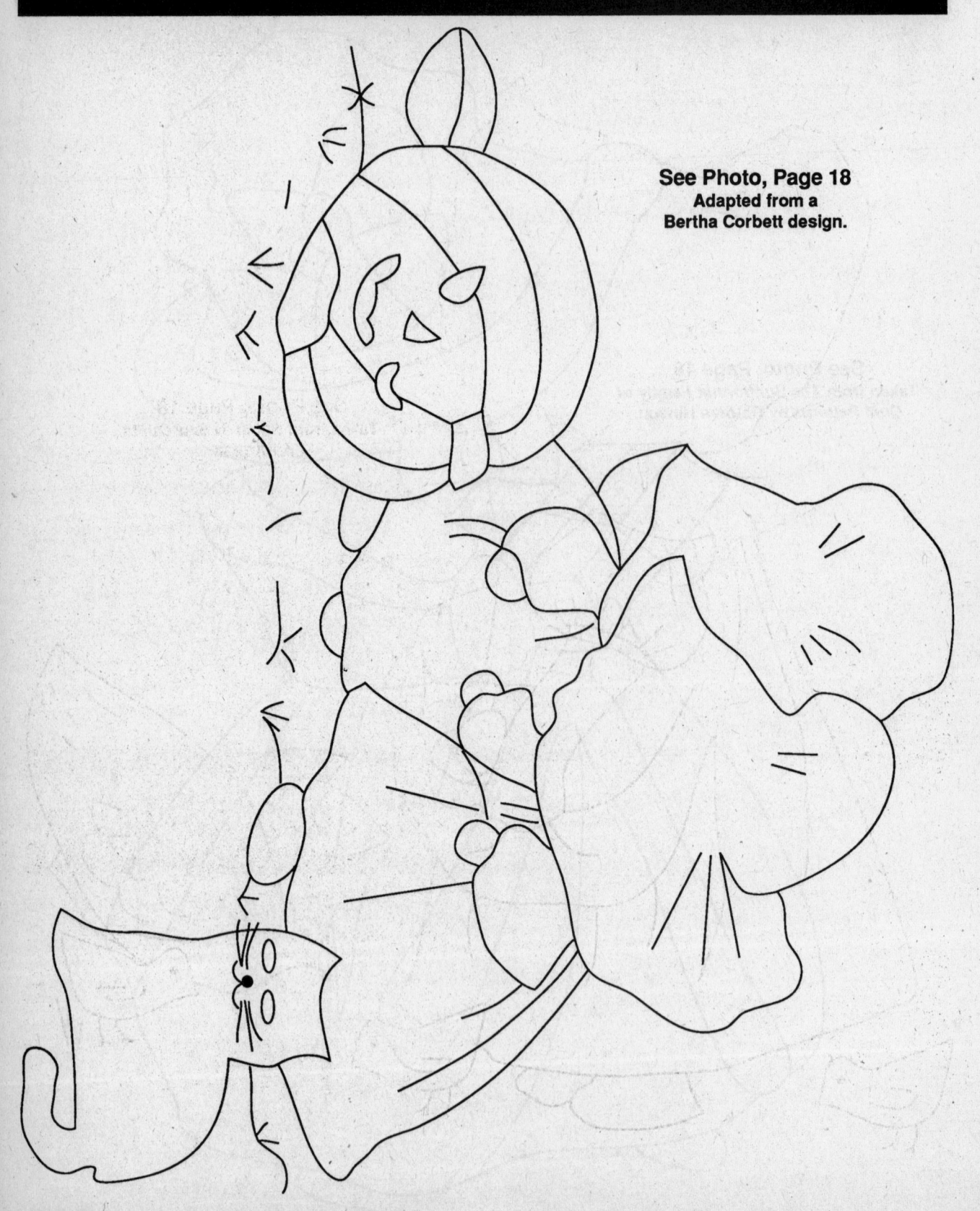

**See Photo, Page 18
Adapted from a
Bertha Corbett design.**

140 Sunbonnet Family Reunion IV

1902 Sunbonnet Molly
Beth S. Vance • Kennewick, WA

Sunbonnet FAMILY REUNION

See Photo, Page 18
Taken from *Stitch 'N Sew Quilts*
April 1988.

Sunbonnet FAMILY REUNION

Painting Day
Elaine Hotra • San Pedro, CA

See Photo, Page 18

142 Sunbonnet Family Reunion IV

Sunbonnet Sue Sunday Best
Dorothy O. Gish • Enterprise, KS

Sunbonnet FAMILY REUNION

See Photo, Page 19

Sunbonnet Family Reunion IV 143

Sunbonnet Ellie
Eloise McCormick • Sherwood, AR

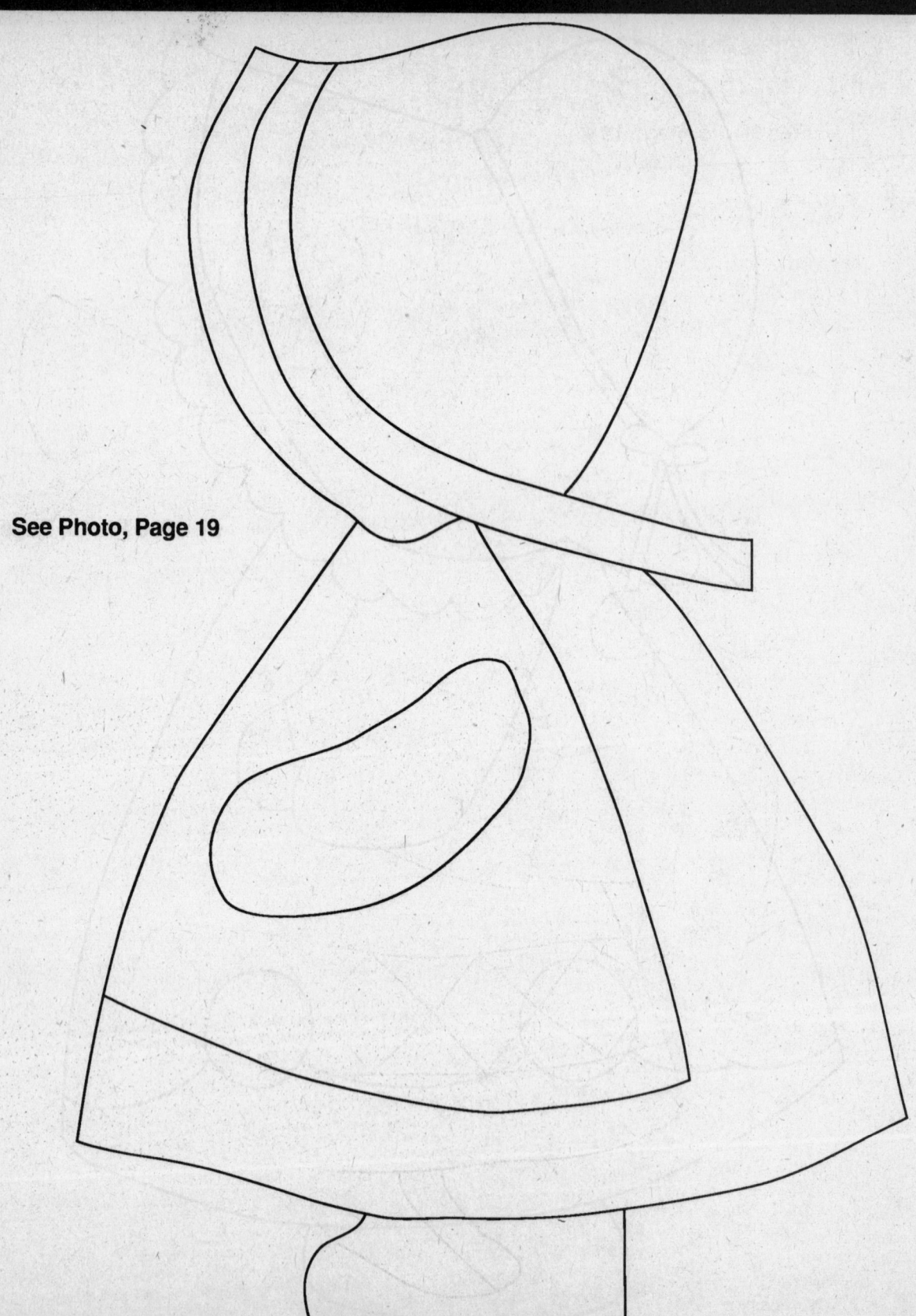

See Photo, Page 19

144 Sunbonnet Family Reunion IV

Sunbonnet Girl Sprinkling
Jacque Moster • Columbus, IN

See Photo, Page 19

Sunbonnet Family Reunion IV

Sunbonnet FAMILY REUNION

Little Modern Shopper
Sheila Shaffer • Phoenix, AZ

See Photo, Page 19
Adapted from *Country Quilts* Summer 1989.

Sunbonnet Family Reunion IV

Paperdoll Sue
Cecelia A. Purciful • Sheridan, IN

See Photo, Page 19

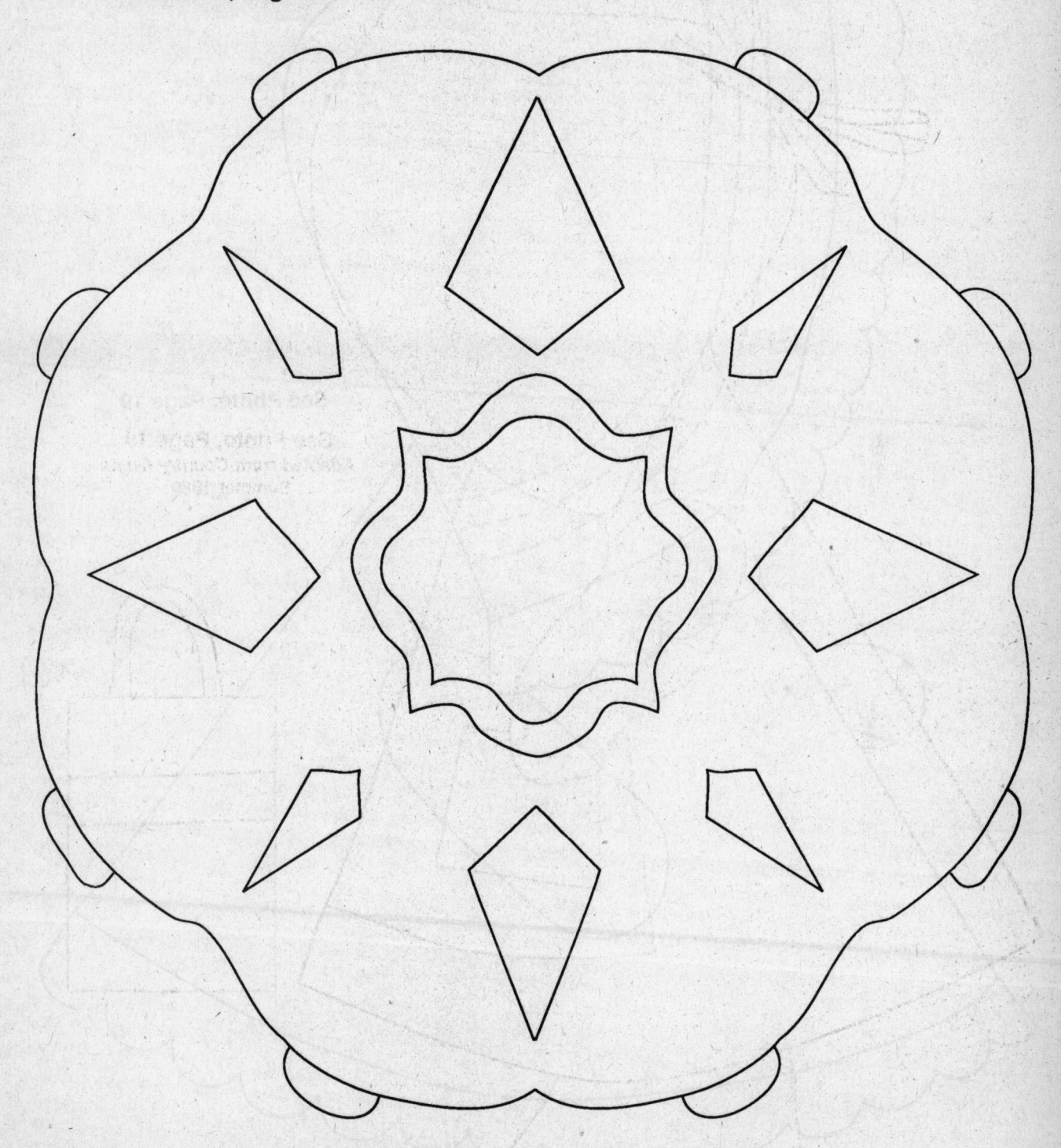

Sunbonnet Family Reunion IV

Sunbonnet FAMILY REUNION

Strike Me Pink
Dorothy Urquhart • Norridgewock, ME

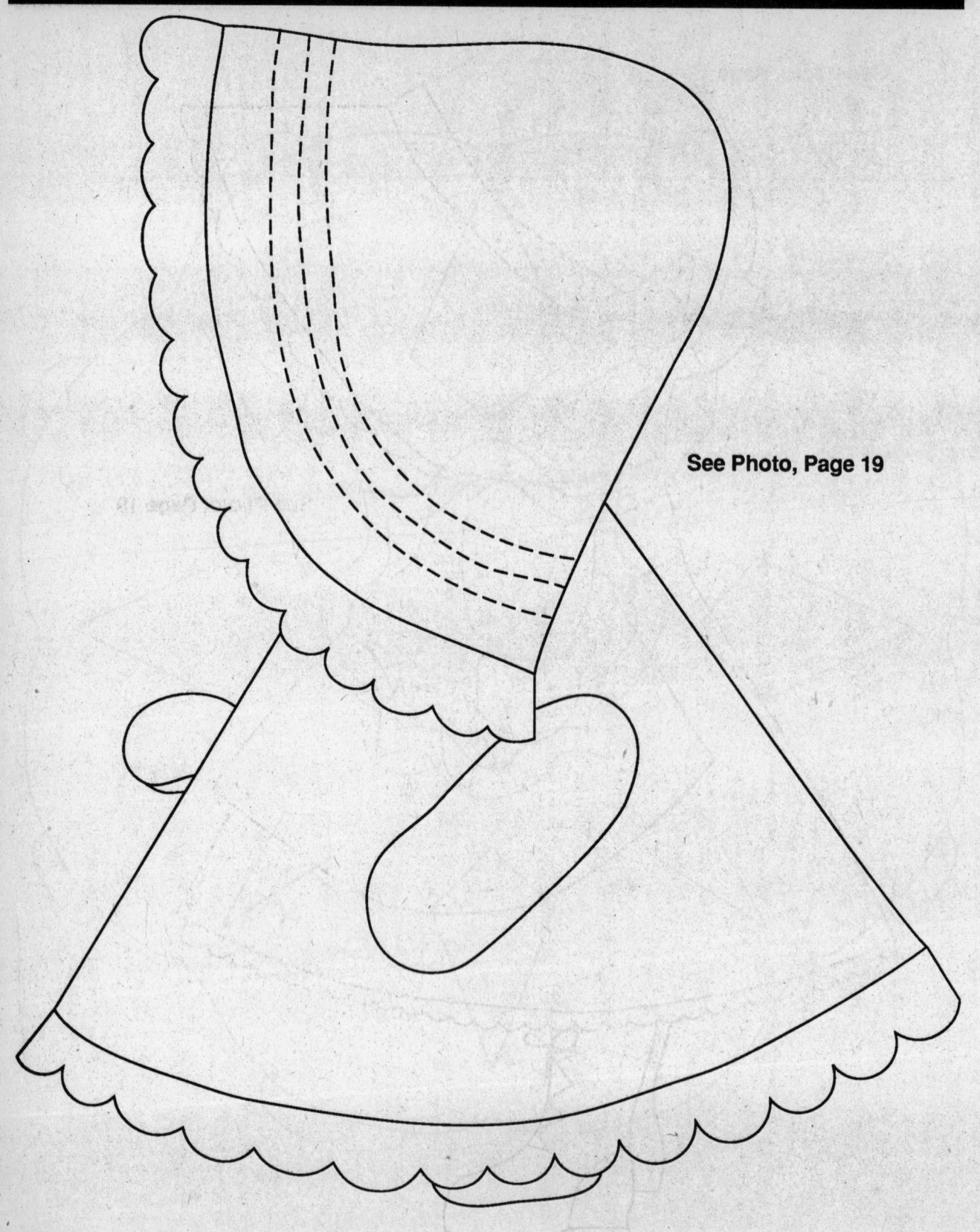

See Photo, Page 19

148 Sunbonnet Family Reunion IV

Hi Top Sue
Maxine Allen • Springfield, MO

Sunbonnet FAMILY REUNION

See Photo, Page 19

Sunbonnet Family Reunion IV 149

Sunbonnet Sue On The Go
Rita Healy • Parma, OH

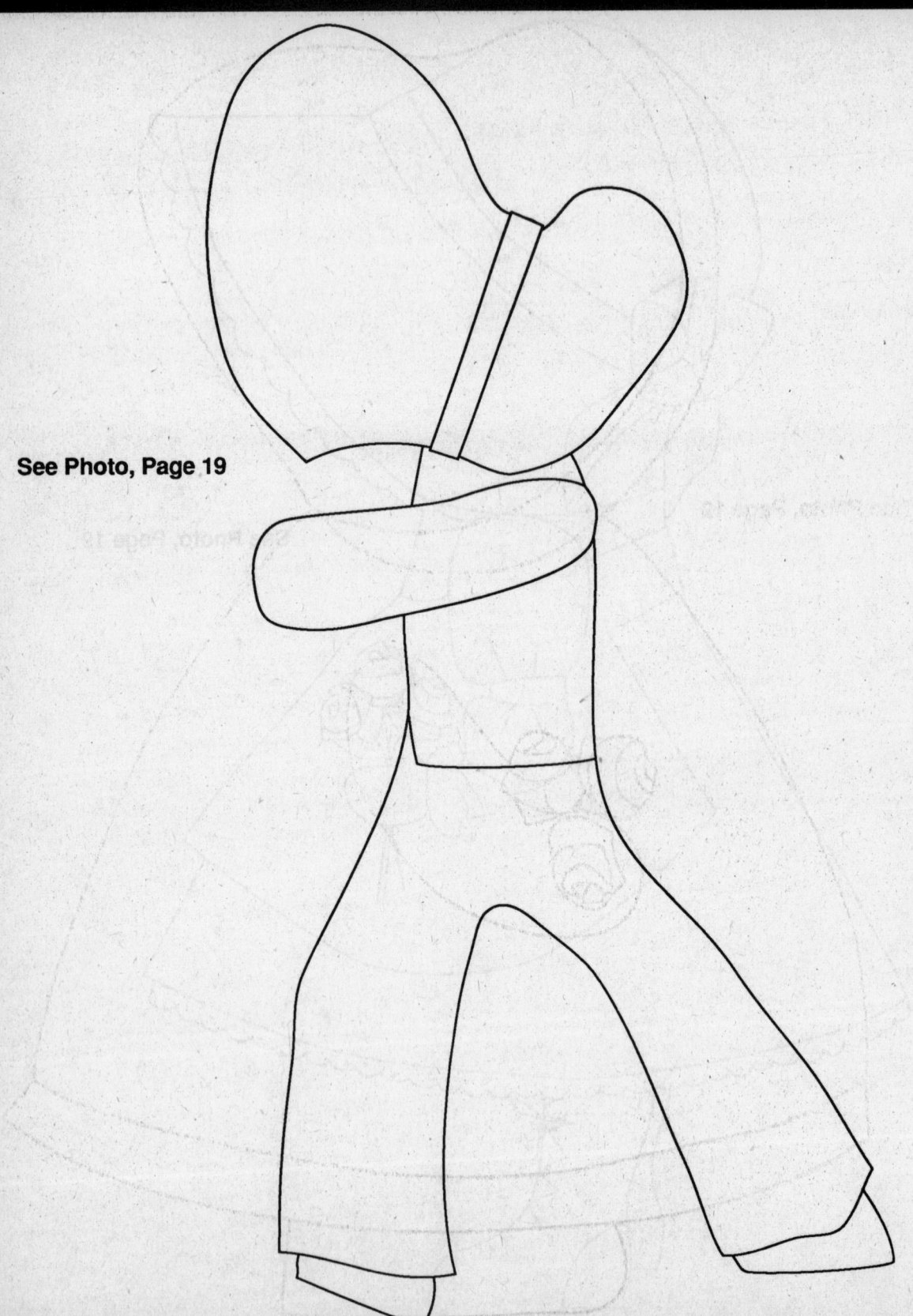

See Photo, Page 19

150 Sunbonnet Family Reunion IV

Giving Love With Flowers
Darlene Jackson • Tallahassee, FL

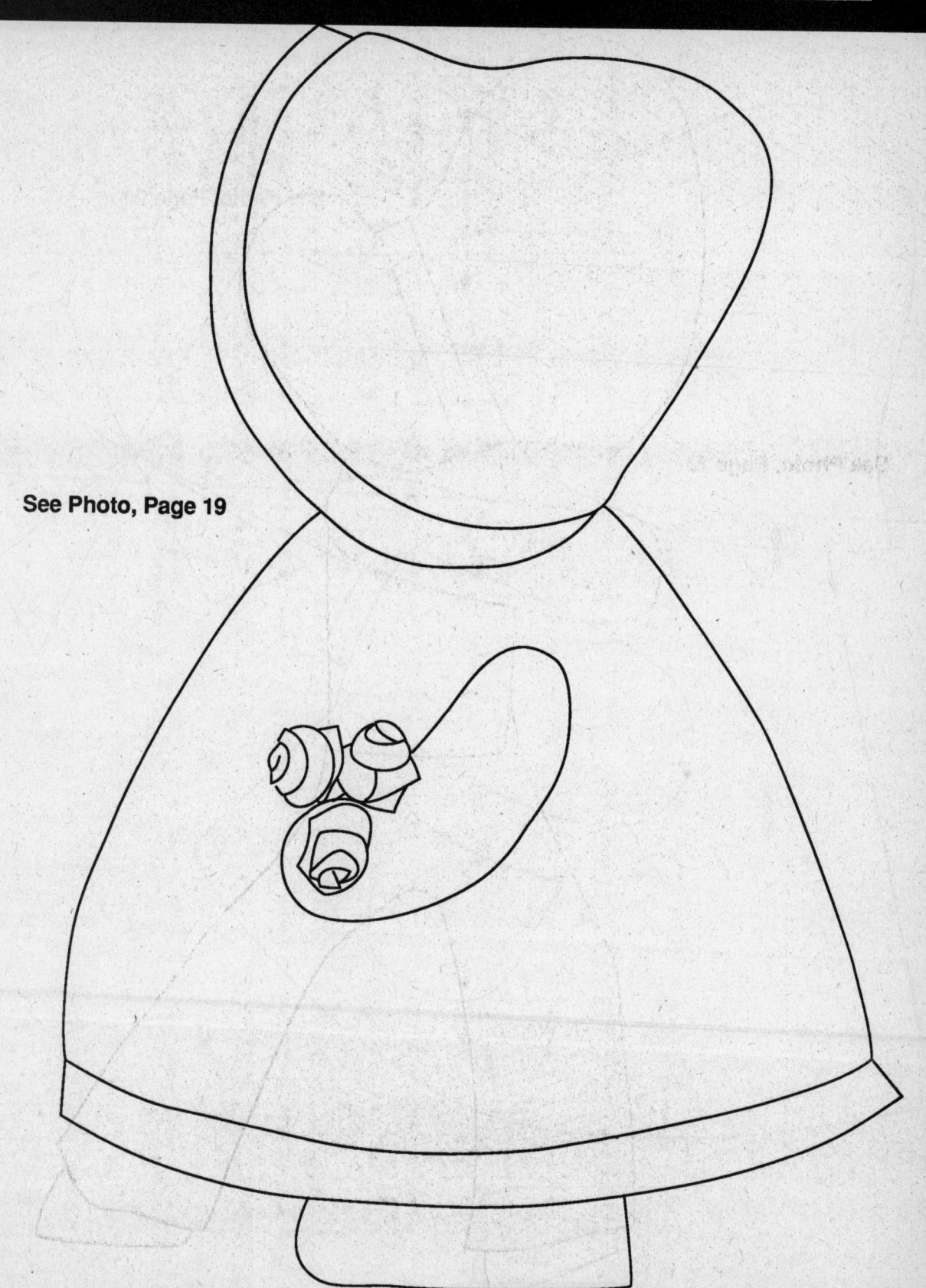

Sunbonnet FAMILY REUNION

See Photo, Page 19

Sunbonnet Family Reunion IV 151

Pinwheel Sue
Rachel R. Campbell • Newport News, VA

See Photo, Page 20

152 Sunbonnet Family Reunion IV

Three Musicians, American Style
Alice G. Noël • St. Louis, MO

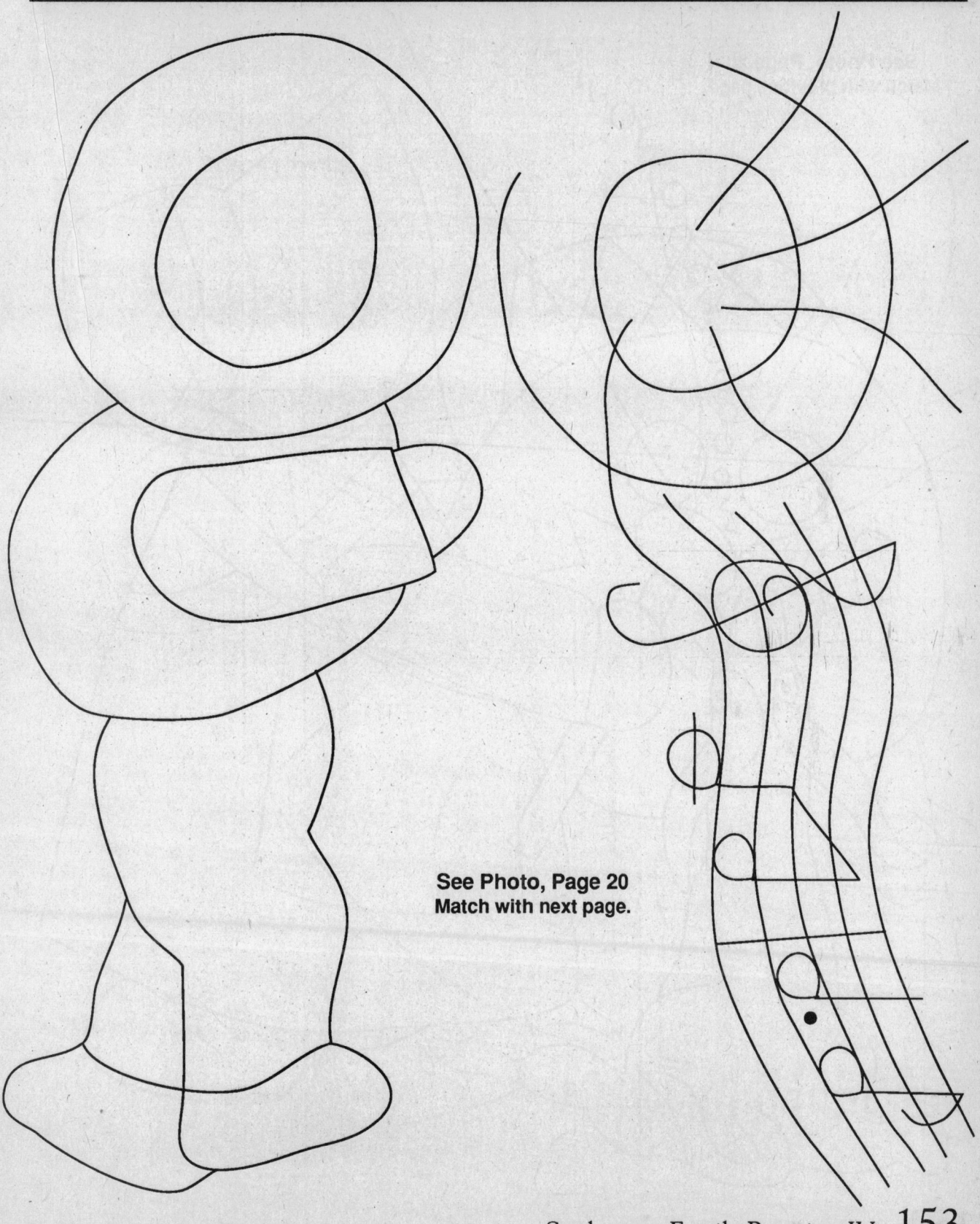

Sunbonnet FAMILY REUNION

See Photo, Page 20
Match with next page.

Sunbonnet Family Reunion IV 153

Sunbonnet
FAMILY REUNION

See Photo, Page 20
Match with previous page.

154 Sunbonnet Family Reunion IV

Picking Berries
Andrea Lamb • Joliet, IL

Sunbonnet FAMILY REUNION

See Photo, Page 20

Sunbonnet Family Reunion IV 155

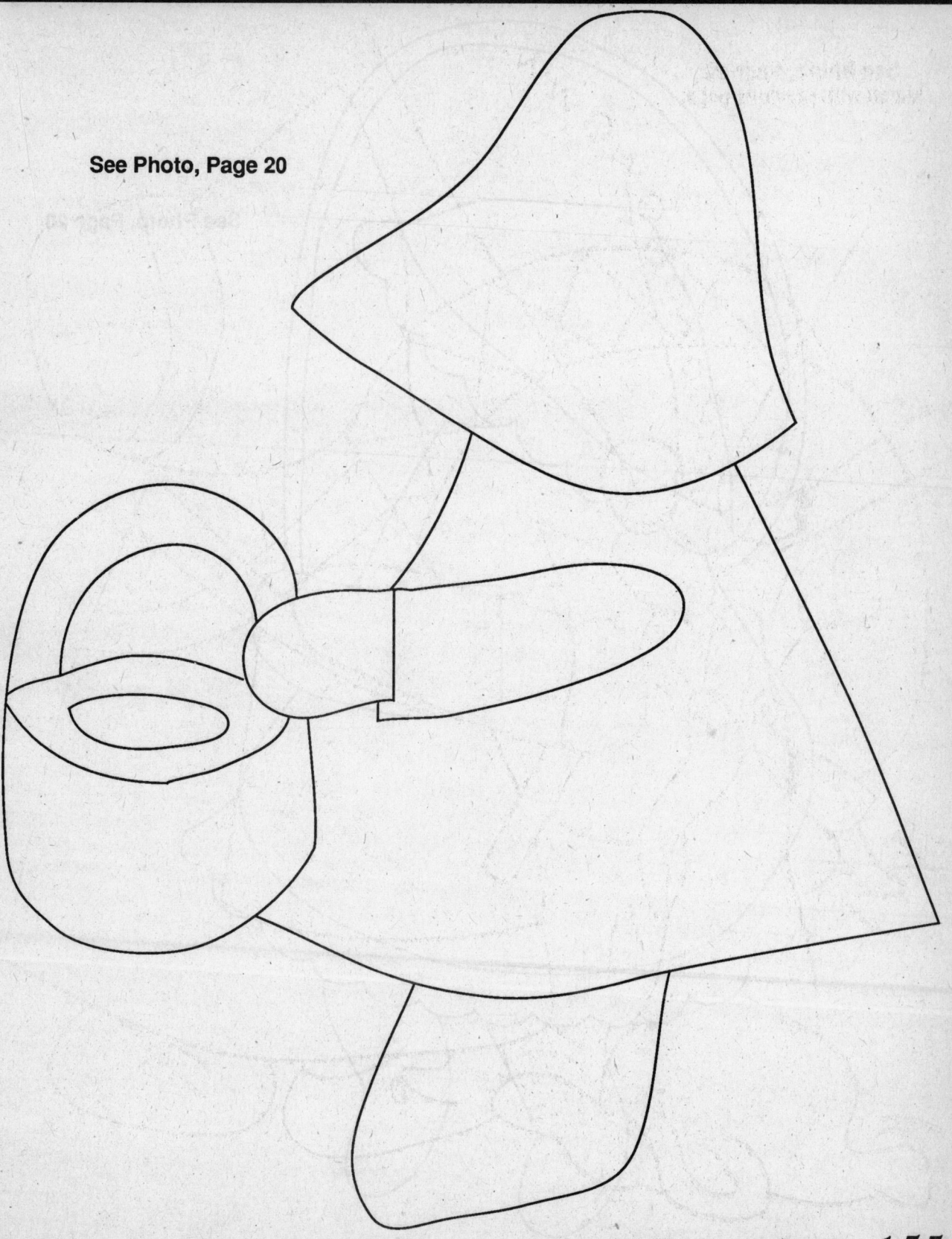

Sunbonnet FAMILY REUNION

Jumping Rope
Sarah Hall • Overland Park, KS

See Photo, Page 20

156 Sunbonnet Family Reunion IV

The Little Drummer Boy
Judith G. Stich • Solana Beach, CA

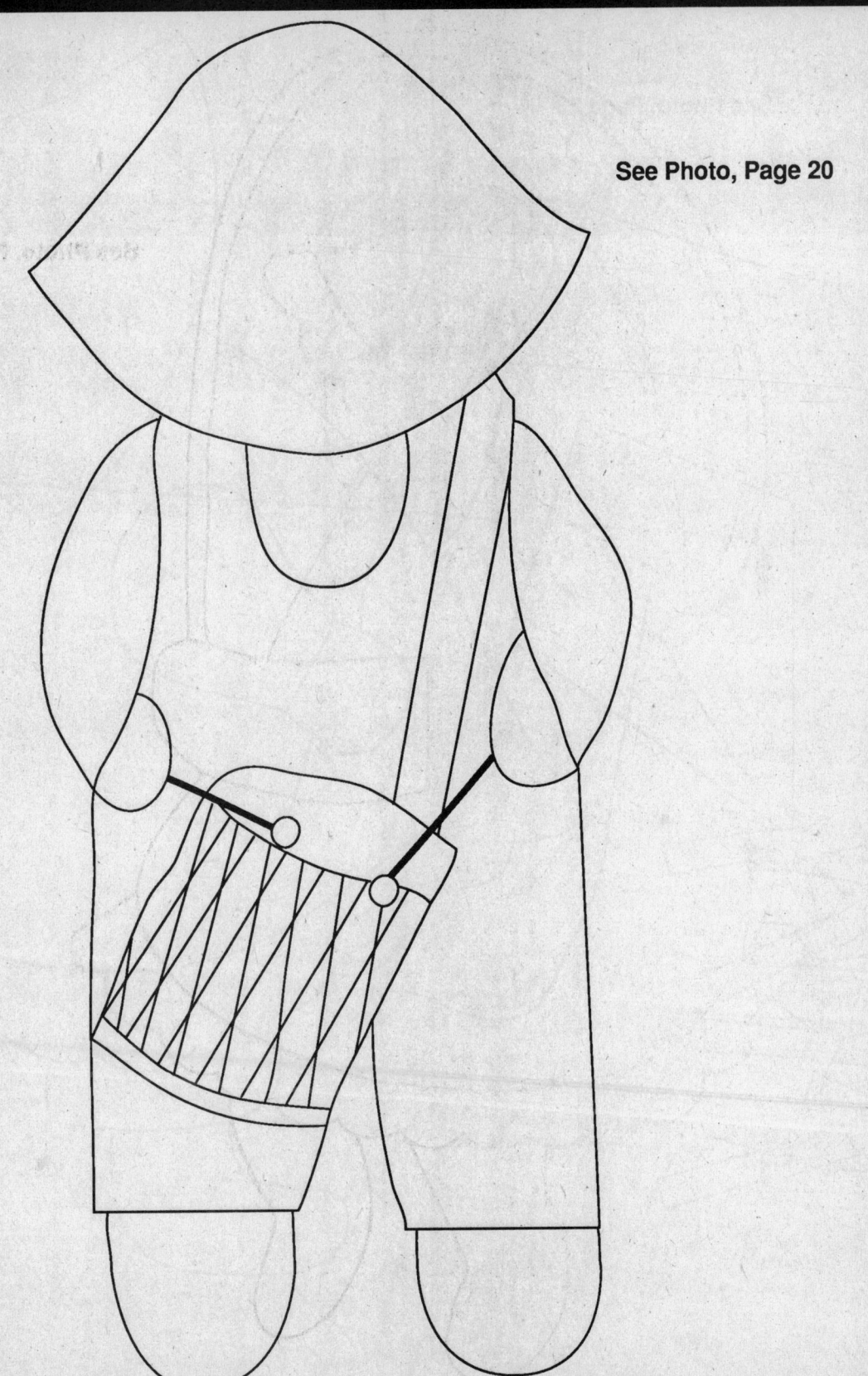

Sunbonnet FAMILY REUNION

See Photo, Page 20

Sunbonnet Family Reunion IV 157

Sunbonnet FAMILY REUNION

Flying High
Vera O'Boyle • Waldorf, MD

See Photo, Page 20

158 Sunbonnet Family Reunion IV

Summer Fun
Ann Pastucha • Peoria, IL

Sunbonnet FAMILY REUNION

See Photo, Page 20

Sunbonnet Family Reunion IV 159

Sunbonnet FAMILY REUNION

My Job Picking The Flowers
Jill Maulik • Riverton, WY

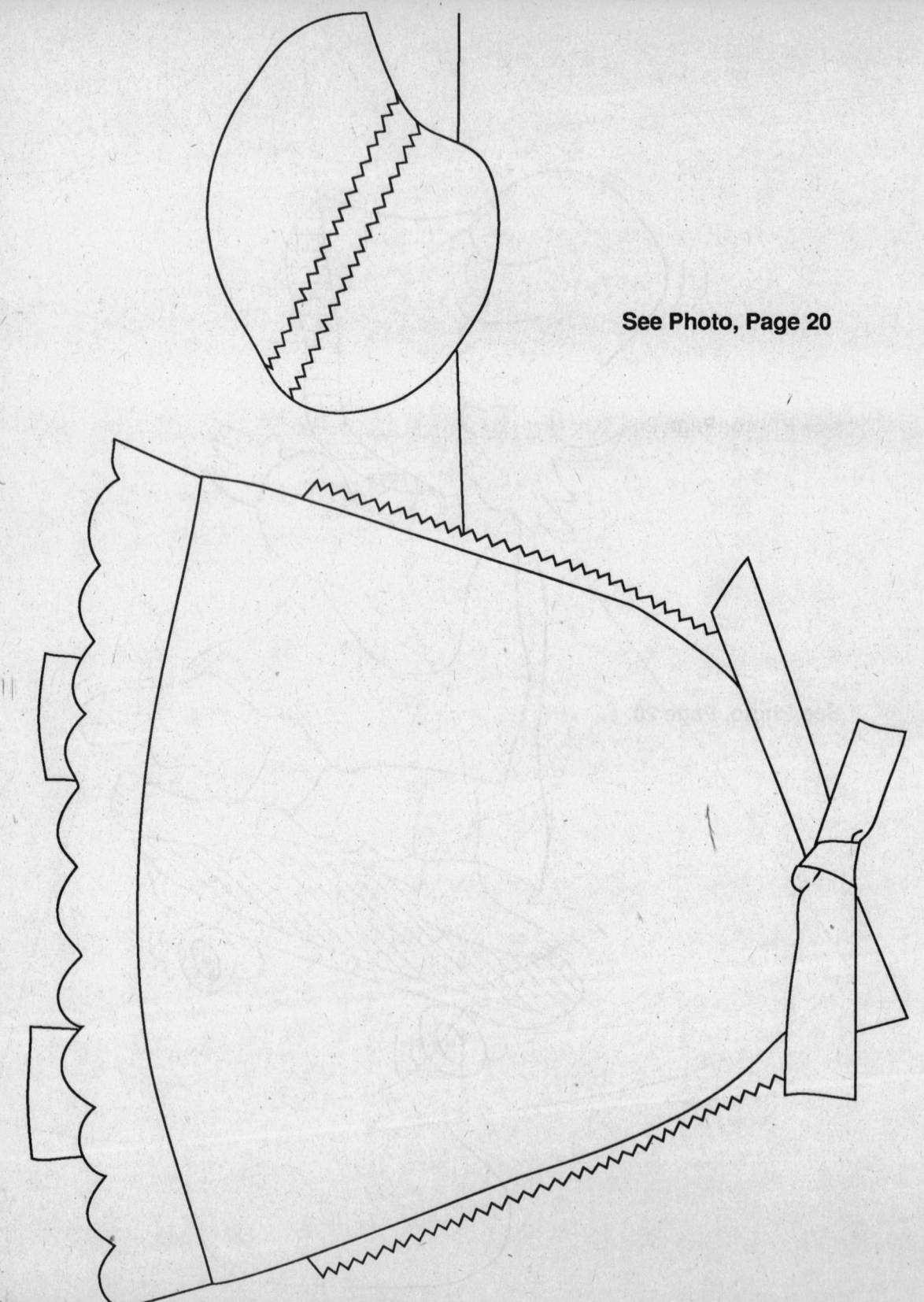

See Photo, Page 20

160   Sunbonnet Family Reunion IV

Kelley's Catch
Linda J. Lewis • Kailua, HI

Sunbonnet FAMILY REUNION

See Photo, Page 20

Sunbonnet Family Reunion IV 161

Sunbonnet FAMILY REUNION

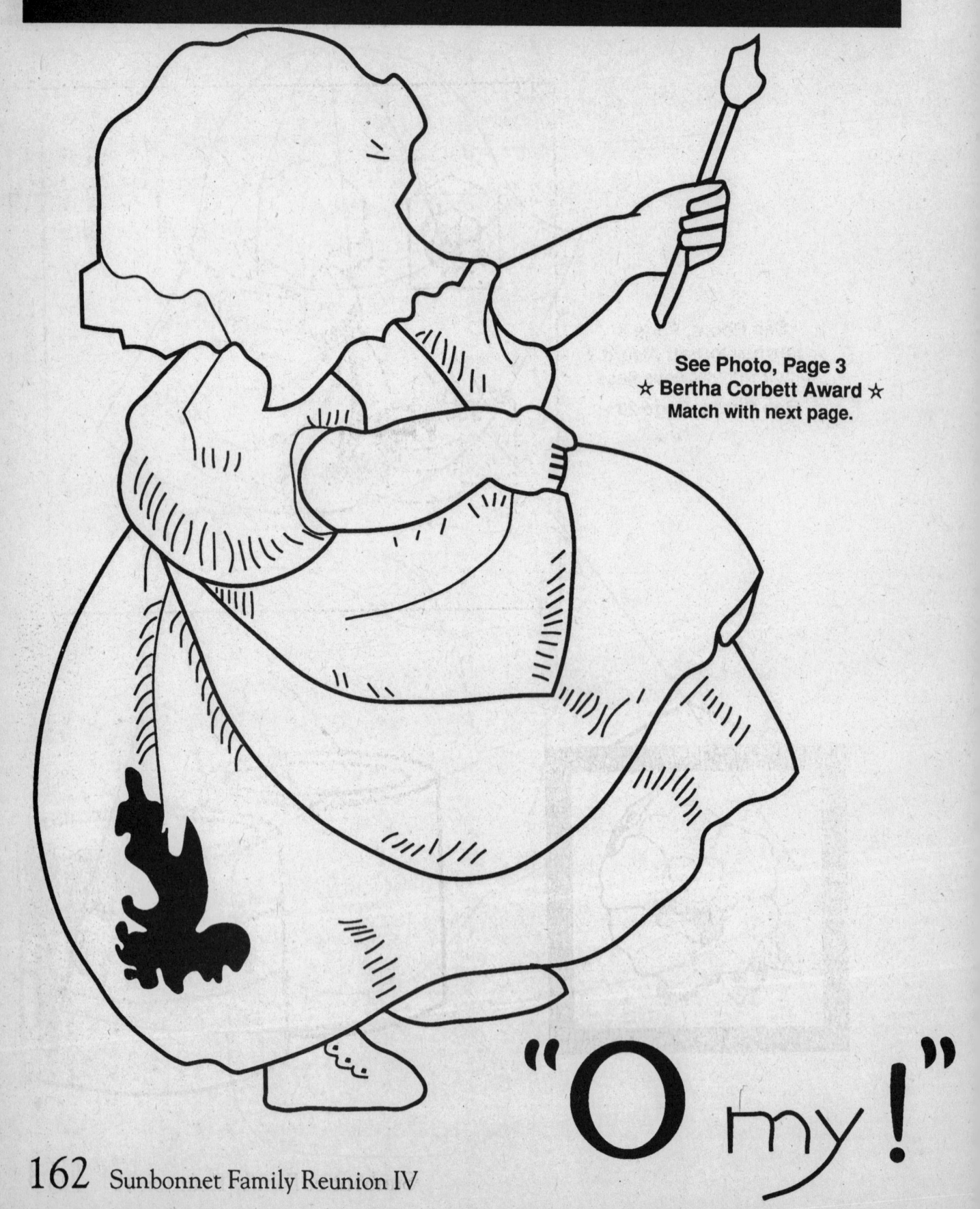

Painting
Norma N. Locke • Gaston, OR

See Photo, Page 3
☆ Bertha Corbett Award ☆
Match with next page.

"O my!"

162   Sunbonnet Family Reunion IV

See Photo, Page 3
☆ Bertha Corbett Award ☆
Match with previous page.

"O my!"

Sunbonnet Family Reunion IV 163

Sunbonnet Family Reunion — INDEX

Name	Location	Page
Hazel L. Abel	Kennewick, WA	108
Jane Allen	Tipp City, OH	124
Maxine Allen	Springfield, MO	149
Hannah Ames	Harvard, IL	116
Patricia Andersen	Lincoln, NE	106,107
Janette Anderson	Irvine, CA	84
Sandra Andrews	Medina, OH	113,114
Rose Marie Baab	Wooster, OH	86
Janie Mountain Baker	Panorama City, CA	71
Jo Barbera	Flemington, NJ	56
Helen Beer	Solon, OH	90
Mary K. Boerger	London, OH	85
Lynda G. Boucke	St. Petersburg, FL	44
Tina Boyd	Live Oak, FL	43
Dorothy Brock	Helena, MT	139
Rachel R. Campbell	Newport News, VA	152
Kit D. Carpenter	Greenwell Springs, LA	140
Ruth Carroll	Patterson, VA	129
Virginia Caudell	Wynne, AR	118
Violet Conley	New Paris, OH	27
Patti Connor	Collinsville, IL	34
I.V. Crawford	Tyler, TX	55
Martie Culp	Wheeling, WV	94
Carol Deal	Bloomington, IL	120
Wanda Debolt	S. Daytona, FL	79
Fae DeWitt	Hoonah, AK	65
Brenda Dodd	Noble, OK	40
Jeanette B. Doerr	Rochester, NY	70
Lorraine Doyle	Kennewick, WA	83
Donna A. Duncan	Eminence, KY	78
Betty Dunlap	Kansas City, MO	135
Georgia Engle	E. Helena, MT	133
Dotty J. Evens	Big Rapids, MI	25
Hazel Frazier	Calumet, OK	99
Opal Frey	Arvada, CO	111
Nova Gaines	Overland Park, KS	82
Dorothy O. Gish	Enterprise, KS	143
Betty Goodwin	Camp Hill, PA	52
Phyllis Graham	Newport News, VA	35
Sarah Hall	Overland Park, KS	156
Rita Healy	Parma, OH	150
Barbara J. Heaton	Park Forest, IL	50
Teresa M. Heinze	Rolla, MO	67
Gail M. Hodge	Garden City, MI	47
Elaine Hotra	San Pedro, CA	142
Darlene Jackson	Tallahassee, FL	151
Carol January	S. Weymouth, MA	45
Elrid Johnson	Brookfield, WI	49
Lucille Johnston	Prairie Village, KS	76
Kathryn A. Jones	Marshall, MO	28
Mary R. Jones	Bulverde, TX	87
Vera Kaiser	Paola, KS	26
Evelyn Kaminsky	Blackwood, NJ	75
Marie M. Kelly	Hemet, CA	68
Ethel B. Kidwell	Kansas City, MO	59
Linda King-Johnson	Barryville, NY	121,122
Jean Klepinger	Greenville, OH	115
Susan N. Knutsen	Emmetsburg, IA	102
Andrea Lamb	Joliet, IL	155
Claudine Langford	Dimmitt, TX	103
Kay Lanham	Lander, WY	91,92
Sharon Larson	The Colony, TX	119
Linda J. Lewis	Kailua, HI	161
Mary Lewis	Locust Grove, OK	131
Norma N. Locke	Gaston, OR	162,163
Cindy Brown Marquardt	Springfield, MO	32
Patti Martinez	Harvard, IL	64
Laura Matkin	San Antonio, TX	38,39
Jill Maulik	Riverton, WY	160
Eloise Lewis McCartney	Poland, OH	72
Margaret McClellan	Osawatomie, KS	42
Sherry L. McConnell	Anderson, IN	134
Eloise McCormick	Sherwood, AR	144
Linda McCuean	New Galilee, PA	97
Lillian Michalez	Vienna, OH	104
Lavina E. Miller	Waterford, NJ	74
Mary Ann Miller	St. Louis, MO	36
Carol A. Miller	Mount Olive, IL	53,54
Melba F. Mitchell	Stanton, CA	117
Jacque Moster	Columbus, IN	145
Alice G. Noël	St. Louis, MO	153,154
Vera O'Boyle	Waldorf, MD	158
Alta M. Parrish	Carmel, IN	61,62
Janet L. Parsons	Monaca, PA	130
Ann Pastucha	Peoria, IL	159
Pat Pierson	Mechanicsburg, PA	58
Francis Pinkerton	Littlefield, TX	66
Leona E. Price	Florissant, MO	98
Cecelia A. Purciful	Sheridan, IN	147
Laura M. Ramseier	Oshkosh, WI	136
Netta Ranney	Overland Park, KS	81
Carol Rhoades	Anchorage, AK	93
Teresa Richard	New York Mills, NY	123
Linda Riedi	DePere, WI	48
Frieda Rippe	Chagrin Falls, OH	29,30
Ruby Rupert	Adrian, MI	73
Phyllis Saelens	Seattle, WA	95
Sybil Scales	Lawrence, KS	100,101
Shari Schmidt	Turpin, OK	57
Pat Scott	Kansas City, MO	77
Karen Searle	Shelley, ID	31
Sheila Shaffer	Phoenix, AZ	146
Tami Shoji	Chatham, Ont., Canada	137,138
Joan Shook	Tombstone, AZ	127
Mickey Singer	Pittsburgh, PA	128
Lois Sours	Drexel, MO	80
Muriel Spencer	Rio Dell, CA	96
Eileen Squitiro	New Milton, WV	41
Victorena Stanis	Westville, IL	112
Judith G. Stich	Solana Beach, CA	157
Cinthia Lou Stolte	McLouth, KS	132
Ardeth Sveadas	Sparta, MI	109,110
Jane Talso	Albuquerque, NM	51
Linda M. Throckmorton	Cutler, ME	89
Sallie Townsend	Westland, MI	69
Ione Trapp	N. Vernon, IN	60
Christine Tucker	Kailua, HI	126
Dorothy Urquhart	Norridgewock, ME	148
Beth S. Vance	Kennewick, WA	141
Pat Vodry	Big Rapids, MI	63
Twila West	Dimmitt, TX	37
Molly Wilson	Gonzales, TX	105
Beatrice J. Woodland	Yreka, CA	88
Marian S. Woods	Central City, IA	33
Eleanor Wright	Santa Barbara, CA	46
Patricia Yerks	Pine Bush, NY	125

NOTES

Now you can have all of Grandma's patterns!
— A QUILT COLLECTOR'S DREAM —
Kansas City Star Classic Quilt Patterns

patterns of yesteryear . . . reprinted for today

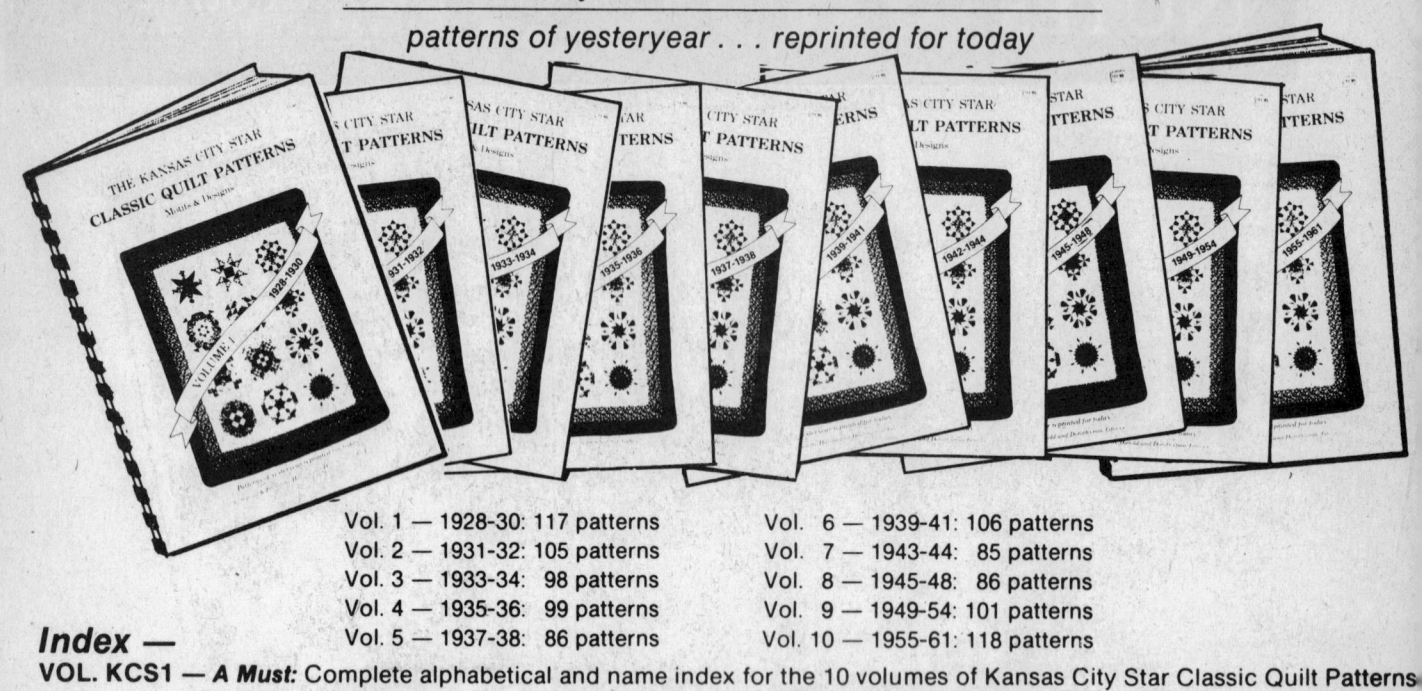

Vol. 1 — 1928-30: 117 patterns
Vol. 2 — 1931-32: 105 patterns
Vol. 3 — 1933-34: 98 patterns
Vol. 4 — 1935-36: 99 patterns
Vol. 5 — 1937-38: 86 patterns
Vol. 6 — 1939-41: 106 patterns
Vol. 7 — 1943-44: 85 patterns
Vol. 8 — 1945-48: 86 patterns
Vol. 9 — 1949-54: 101 patterns
Vol. 10 — 1955-61: 118 patterns

Index —
VOL. KCS1 — *A Must:* Complete alphabetical and name index for the 10 volumes of Kansas City Star Classic Quilt Patterns

MORE PATTERNS OF YESTERYEAR . . .

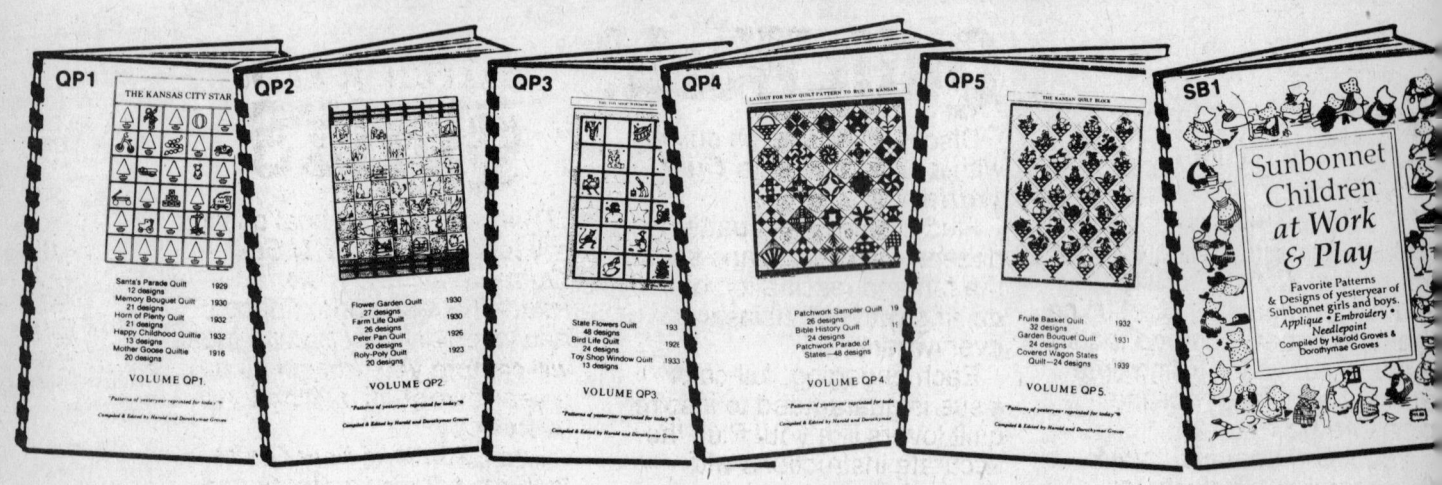

VOL. QP1	Year	# designs
Santa's Parade Quilt	1929	12
Memory Bouquet Quilt	1930	21
Horn of Plenty Quilt	1932	21
Happy Childhood Quiltie	1932	13
Mother Goose Quiltie	1916	20
VOL. QP2	**Year**	**# designs**
Flower Garden Quilt	1930	27
Farm Life Quilt	1930	26
Peter Pan Quilt	1926	20
Roly-Poly Quilt	1923	20
VOL. QP3	**Year**	**# designs**
State Flowers Quilt	1931	48
Bird Life Quilt	1928	24
Toy Shop Window Quilt	1933	13

VOL. QP4	Year	# designs
Patchwork Sampler Quilt	1930	2
Bible History Quilt	1927	2
Patchwork Parade of States	1931	4
VOL. QP5	**Year**	**# designs**
Fruite Basket Quilt	1932	3
Garden Bouquet Quilt	1931	2
Covered Wagon States	1939	2

VOL. SB1
Sunbonnet Children at Work & Play
Favorite Sunbonnets *(Grandma's Collection)*
Favorite Patterns & Designs of yesteryear of Sunbonnet girls and boys.
Applique — Embroidery — Needlepoint

Only complete collection of its kind (over 1400 patterns) • Spiral Bound • Order individually or all
$12.95 each ($2.50 postage & handling each) Postage paid on orders of 5 or more volumes
Orders: VISA or MasterCard (Dealers welcomed!)

Groves Publishing Co.
P.O. Box 5370   Kansas City, MO 64131

Order today! Patterns Grandma loved!

When ordering please enclose your UPS address.

A QUILTING TRIO!

Quick & Easy Quilting

Fast, fun quilting projects are yours with **Quick & Easy Quilting** magazine! Start using the techniques, tips and tools that will cut your quilting time and enhance your quilting pleasure now!

You'll find beautiful, quick (but creative!) projects for quilts, wall hangings, place mats, apparel and more. **Subscribe today!**

Quilt World

Discover the best in quilting with a subscription to *Quilt World* magazine!

Find creative quilt patterns for dozens of projects, and share the fun and fascination of quilting with enthusiasts everywhere.

Each engaging, full-color issue is guaranteed to inspire quilt lovers like you! Plus the accurate instructions with detailed diagrams make beautiful quilting oh-"sew"-easy!

Start your subscription today!

STITCH 'N SEW QUILTS

The best of traditional quilting is yours with **Stitch 'N Sew Quilts,** issue after colorful issue! Big, bold, bright photos and loads of great quilting ideas will capture your imagination – a year's worth of quilting fun in every copy!

Each *Stitch 'n Sew Quilts* features full-size patterns and charts. Subscribe today and your quilting projects will go ever "sew" smoothly!

Mark your choices here:

- ☐ *Quick & Easy Quilting* (1 year, 4 issues) $9.95
- ☐ *Quilt World* (1 year, 6 issues) $12.97
- ☐ *Stitch 'N Sew Quilts* (1 year, 6 issues) $12.97

☐ Bill Me Later   New Subscriber ☐
☐ Payment Enclosed   Renewal ☐
☐ Visa   ☐ MasterCard   ☐ Check

CARD NO. _____   MC Interbank No. _____

Signature _____   Expiration Date _____

Clip this coupon today and mail it to:
Quilt Subscriptions
P.O. Box 11302, Des Moines, IA 50340.

Your Name _____
Address _____
City / State / Zip _____

EXPIRES 5/92   D097

—Collectible patterns for quilters!—

SUNBONNET SUE ALBUMS
family reunion!

Get all four big books for only $49.95!
While supply lasts!

SBFR, 306 East Parr Road
Berne, Indiana 46711

Your Name _____
Address _____
City / State / Zip _____

EXPIRES 5/92   D096

Mark your Sunbonnet Album *choices* here. U.S. funds only. No cash, stamps or CODs please. Canadians please add to postage & handling charges.

☐ **Album Set** — **4 Album set** $49.95 plus $2.50 p&h
☐ **Album I** — **Any 1 Album** $14.95 plus $1.50 p&h
☐ **Album II**
☐ **Album III** — **Any 2 Albums** $27.50 plus $1.50 p&h
☐ **Album IV*** — **Any 3 Albums** $39.95 plus $2 p&h

*Album IV will be mailed in June, 9

Imagine! A collection of over 500 warm and cheerful Sunbonnets can now be yours for only a dime per full-size pattern!

Each of the four volumes in this set has 126 full-size, prize-winning Sunbonnet patterns—plus a detailed full-color photograph of each finished block. You'll love the easy-to-follow instructions for making and showing each of your favorite blocks! And you'll get some fascinating history about Bertha Corbett, the mother of Sunbonnets, and her family!

You can order one or all of these collectible pattern books and complete your Sunbonnet library today!

Fill out the coupon above, select your Sunbonnet Albums and enclose full payment. We'll mail your order right away.

Your satisfaction is completely guaranteed. If after looking over your new collection you are dissatisfied for any reason, just mail the books back to us for a refund! Hurry, order your complete set today!

OVER 500 FULL-SIZE SUNBONNET PATTERNS!

Sunbonnet — FAMILY REUNION — Album I

Sunbonnet — FAMILY REUNION — Album II

Sunbonnet — FAMILY REUNION — Album III

Sunbonnet — FAMILY REUNION — Album IV